WOMEN IN SOCIETY
A Feminist List edited by
Jo Campling

Editorial Advisory Group

Phillida Bunckle, *Victoria University, Wellington, New Zealand;*
Miriam David, *South Bank University;* Leonore Davidoff,
University of Essex; Janet Finch, *University of Lancaster;*
Jalna Hanmer, *University of Bradford;* Beverley Kingston,
University of New South Wales, Australia; Hilary Land, *University
of Bristol;* Diana Leonard, *University of London Institute of
Education;* Susan Lonsdale, *South Bank University;* Jean O'Barr,
Duke University, North Carolina, USA; Arlene Tigar McLaren,
Simon Fraser University, British Columbia, Canada; Hilary Rose,
University of Bradford; Susan Sellers, *Centre D'Etudes Feminines,
Université de Paris;* Pat Thane, *Goldsmiths' College, University of
London;* Clare Ungerson, *University of Kent at Canterbury.*

The last 20 years have seen an explosion of publishing by, about
and for women. This new list is designed to make a particular
contribution to this continuing process by commissioning and
publishing books which consolidate and advance feminist research
and debate in key areas in a form suitable for students, academics
and researchers but also accessible to a broader general readership.

As far as possible, books will adopt an international perspective
incorporating comparative material from a range of countries where
this is illuminating. Above all they will be interdisciplinary, aiming
to put women's studies and feminist discussion firmly on the agenda
in subject-areas as disparate as law, literature, art and social policy.

A list of published and forthcoming titles follows overleaf

Learning Resources
Centre

Women and Disability

The Experience of Physical Disability among Women

Susan Lonsdale

MACMILLAN

362.4082
LON

First published 1990 by
THE MACMILLAN PRESS LTD
Houndmills, Basingstoke, Hampshire RG21 2XS
and London
Companies and representatives
throughout the world

ISBN 0–333–42666–5 hardcover
ISBN 0–333–42667–3 paperback

A catalogue record for this book is available
from the British Library.

Reprinted 1992, 1994

Printed in China

Series Standing Order

If you would like to receive future titles in this series as they are published, you can
make use of our standing order facility. To place a standing order please contact your
bookseller or, in case of difficulty,write to us at the address below with your name
and address and the name of the series. Please state with which title you wish to
begin your standing order. (If you live outside the United Kingdom we may not have
the rights for your area, in which case we will forward your order to the publisher
concerned.)

Customer Services Department, Macmillan Distribution Ltd
Houndmills, Basingstoke, Hampshire RG21 2XS, England

22.8.95

For my mother and father

Contents

Preface

For some time I have been interested in the effects of physical impairment and disability on ordinary women and men. Having a disability often gives people a minority status, fundamentally affecting their life chances and their ability to live the kind of life they might otherwise have expected to lead – not least of all because of discrimination in the crucial areas of education and employment. I have also had an interest for many years in the roles that women play in our society and the extent to which gender influences the choices they make and the lifestyles they lead. While technically not a minority group as such, women often experience similar processes of disadvantage and discrimination. I became interested, therefore, to see what happened when these two characteristics coincided; to see how women with physical disabilities experienced a double disadvantage and what strategies they developed to deal with their situation. I felt that as women, they would be particularly susceptible to prejudices about physical disability and its effects, but that they would also have developed an armoury of inventive strategies for dealing with disadvantage.

I judged that the best way of beginning such a task was to spend some time with women who were disabled. I therefore undertook detailed interviews with twenty-two women of different ages, races and socio-economic backgrounds. All had one thing in common: they had experienced physical or sensory disability which had not arisen out of a natural process of ageing. They were all of working age. I spent many hours with them, asking some structured questions about their personal lives and discussing more generally with them the political and economic consequences of being disabled. I spoke to women who had been born with their disability, women who had become disabled as children, and women who had developed a disability later in their adult lives. All were extremely generous with their time. I spent many mornings, afternoons and evenings talking to them, and am greatly indebted to them. These interviews and conversations were an important catalyst which stimulated and influenced both my own views and my understanding of other research. This book will present their views within a more general review of the effects of physical disability with particular reference to women.

I did not wish to restrict the study to any particular type of disability, as my interest was not in the disability itself, but in the effect of *any* form of physical disability on women. In other words, I wished the focus to be on the women as a group experiencing physical disablement in a society which has certain views about the role of women and certain norms about physical appearance. It therefore became important to include women with a variety of different types of physical disabilities to assess if there were any common features or differences in their experience. While recognising that different types of disability have different consequences in terms of the specifics of day-to-day functioning, I was rather more interested to place physical disability into a social and political context to ascertain the general significance that gender plays in the process of being or becoming disabled.

SUSAN LONSDALE

Acknowledgements

Books are never the private endeavours of one person. This book could not have been written without help given by a great many people, some without realising it over the years, others more recently by their willingness to talk about it and read through it. I am particularly grateful to Jo Campling for her pioneering work in this field and for all her encouragement and support throughout the task of writing. There are a number of other people who I would also like to thank: Nicole Davoud and Jane Nation, who helped a great deal by reading a draft of the book – although I did not always take their advice, and must bear responsibility for what has finally emerged, their comments and suggestions were invaluable; Mary Lonsdale for many insights shared with me; Mary Davies, Frances Hasler, Rachel Hurst, Anjana Nathwani and Pat Rock for giving me their time and advice when I first embarked on the book; Jenny Altschuler for drawing my attention to issues confronting mothers who have disabilities; Mary Croxon John for some interesting discussions; Sonia Lane for transcribing endless tapes; the many women who have encouraged me with sisterhood and friendship over the years; and most importantly, the women who I met for the first time when interviewing for this book, who were generous and helpful far beyond that which I could have expected. As always, my greatest debt is to Stan Newman, who never stopped believing I could do it.

S.L.

1

Introduction

Most women with disabilities live ordinary lives and face the same daily dilemmas as everyone else. They go to school or college, they live in the community, they have jobs and careers. They fall in love, have sexual relationships, bear children, have friendships, and have the same needs to visit these friends, go to the cinema or go out for a meal. In order to do these things, however, they often have to show considerable strength of purpose in overcoming obstacles of segregation, inaccessible buildings, arrogant professionals, and an image of disability which is negative and demeaning and sets them apart from the rest of the world.

To be disabled, therefore, is also to be disadvantaged. It means regularly being unable to participate in the social and economic activities which most people take for granted. It means confronting the negative attitudes of others and sometimes internalising those negative reactions until they become part of the psychological accoutrements of disability itself. However, at the same time it can also mean gaining the additional insight that comes from encountering a wider range of experiences. It can mean overcoming enormous challenges, leading to a sense of achievement and fulfilment. It can mean a sense of solidarity with other oppressed people and the emergence of a social and political community of people with disabilities.

While this applies to people with both physical and mental disabilities, the focus of this book will be on women with physical or sensory disabilities. The term 'physical disability' will be used to include all forms of disability, including sensory disabilities, which arise out of physical impairments. It excludes psychiatric disorders or intellectual disabilities (the latter often referred to as mental handicap), although much of the discussion will also apply to people experiencing them, particularly when multiple handicaps are present.

There is a great deal of controversy over the word 'disabled'. Some have argued that it is a pejorative, blanket term which is used to refer to a large number of people who have nothing in common except that they do not function in exactly the same way as people who are called 'normal' or 'ablebodied'. This school of thought sees it as a stigmatising label which leads to people with disabilities being excluded from all spheres of social life. To be called 'the disabled' is also seen eventually to lead those so named into a state of conditioned passivity (Brisenden, 1986, p. 175: Sutherland, 1981, p. 15). Others have accepted that this process of labelling and discrimination occurs but, nonetheless, have continued to use the concept of 'disabled people' as an accurate description of a social minority (Safilios-Rothschild, 1970; Oliver, 1986). In this context, it is seen to encourage feelings of solidarity, strength and supportiveness among a group of people whose disparate physical characteristics are uniformly used to oppress them – rather like the slogan 'black is beautiful' was used to turn around a negative concept in the 1960s. These writers view disability as a particular form of social oppression in which socio-economic and political forces impinge upon and restrict the lives of certain people (Oliver, 1983, 1986; Duval, 1984).

Oppression here is taken to refer to a situation in which one group of people systematically undermines another group materially and psychologically, thus invalidating the experiences of the oppressed group. This leads to discrimination, which may be facilitated if the subject group internalises the myths and stereotypes generated about it. Physical disability entails 'the burden of passive oppression' (Campling, 1981a, p. 52) in the following respect. Much of the rejection experienced is not overtly hostile (although it can and does sometimes become so) but comprises a consistently low and patronising expectation of the person with the disability. This results in practical and material deprivation for those who experience it, e.g. lack of accessibility and loss of income. It also has symbolic meanings for people. For instance, the more physical appearance according to an idealised norm is highly valued, the more difficult it will be to live with a physical disability; whereas in societies which perceive certain physical traits to be manifestations of spiritual power, e.g. epilepsy, the less difficult it will be.

For the purpose of this book, the phrase 'people with disabilities', or more often 'women with disabilities', will more generally be used. This enables us to retain the concept of disability without suggesting that a particular physical attribute embodies all there is to know about a person. A key premise upon which this analysis is based is that the concept of disability needs to be understood as a social construct. This means that disablement is something more than just an individual problem. It has a social context in which certain meanings are attributed to having a disability. As Scott has shown in his study of blind men, 'Blindness . . . is a social role that people who have shown difficulty seeing or who cannot see at all must learn how to play' (Scott, 1969, p. 3). Similarly, babies born with a certain genotype such as being female are socialised into particular sex roles. Both social roles have a profound effect on the life chances of the individuals, both objectively in what is on offer for them and subjectively in terms of what they perceive themselves to be capable. To understand what it means to be a woman with a disability requires an analysis of the confluence of these two forms of socialisation in one individual. There are obviously other significant dimensions to this process such as class and race (Confederation of Indian Organisations, 1988).

Women and physical appearance

Physical appearance has long been recognised as something which has particular relevance to women. Women in Western society are required to conform to an image which is based on certain sexual, physical and behavioural stereotypes (which also often imply certain cultural and material lifestyles). This image may change over time as the fashion and make-up industry determines, but it is always there, providing a model or ideal type to which most women aspire and work towards achieving. Magazines, television and advertising convey the image. Industries provide the goods and services to help women create themselves in that image. The stereotype is usually extremely difficult to attain naturally, without the aid of the cosmetics industry, hairdressers and dieting. In their search for this Holy Grail of Beauty, some women will undergo surgery to change an awkward nose, to remove the lines of ageing, or to increase the size of their breasts.

For some women, the ideal is difficult if not impossible to attain. If a woman is very short or very tall, or if she has a prominent feature on her face or body, it will be more difficult to reach. For other women, the ideal is impossible. Someone who uses calipers or a wheelchair cannot walk on stiletto heels; someone with facial scarring or disfigurement cannot look like the advertisements for make-up; and someone with scoliosis or who is born without arms or legs cannot approximate Marilyn Monroe.

For women, there is a premium attached to looking a certain way. And that premium is linked to finding a male partner or husband. It does not matter that we *know* that while very few women look like the ideal, most women do get married or cohabit with men at some stage during their lives. The power of the image lies in the irrational effect that it has on women and how it influences their aspirations. The things that women *do* to themselves are usually in order to make themselves look attractive according to this powerful image. The make-up they put on, the diets they follow, the clothes they wear represent the less harmful aspects of this behaviour. Anorexia, bulimia, and wearing spine-harming stilettos represent the life-threatening or dangerous aspects of this behaviour.

A small example which illustrates this came from a woman who was interviewed for this book. She was in her early twenties, wore callipers and walked with a crutch. She hated the effect this had on her appearance and the distortion she felt it created on her body shape. She felt ugly and unattractive. Consequently, she made a very significant decision regarding her life. Although she knew that it was physiologically better for her health to keep walking as long as possible to get the exercise, she exchanged crutch and callipers for a wheelchair. This way, she felt she could glide quietly and gracefully into a room, and look less distorted. Probably most importantly, she reported experiencing a great difference in other people's interactions with her. She felt they could cope better with a woman perceived to be more dependent and 'helpless' in a wheelchair than with a woman perceived to be clumsy, or 'ugly' and possibly more assertive in callipers.

The premium attached to *looking* a certain way for women is also manifested in the signals we receive about how we should *not look*. We are all familiar with the ways in which 'ugly' women are portrayed. From their very early days, little girls are taught to associate 'ugliness' with nastiness. Cinderella's two ugly sisters try to create unhappiness for which they ultimately pay the heavy penalty of spinsterhood. Hansel and Gretel's wicked witch is usually portrayed as a hunchbacked elderly woman walking with a stick. Virtually all the traditional fairy stories contain this message alongside the pretty, blonde, white heroines that are Cinderella, Sleeping Beauty, Snow White, and so on. We are systematically taught to hate and fear darkness, old age and disability, equating them with 'ugliness' and to strive after 'prettiness', youth, fair hair and whiteness.

Self-image

A significant part of self-image or the internal conception people have of themselves is made up of their body image, i.e. what their physical appearance means to them and how they believe they appear to others. The centrality of body image in determining self-esteem varies from person to person. It is more likely to be important, for instance, to a woman who is considered and believes herself to be beautiful or to people who pride themselves on being physically fit. It is certainly more likely to be important to women than to men, given the emphasis that is placed on women's physical appearance.

When a woman is born with a disability it will usually be incorporated into her self-image. Since she is not immune to dominant values about beauty and physical appearance, however, her self-image is likely to suffer the further she perceives herself to be from those standards (Nathan, 1977; Hopper, 1981). If a woman becomes disabled she may have to reassess her self-image. It may initially be a negative and stressful experience, since being previously without a disability, she is just as likely as everyone else to have internalised the dominant values about physical attractiveness. Even if is she is young and has not strongly internalised them, the changes she will experience both practically and in terms of her interpersonal relations can affect her perception of herself (Safilios-Rothschild,

1970, p. 96). Some studies have documented the latter in terms of the stigmatising or inhibited and overcontrolled ways in which people without disabilities interact with those with a disability (Comer and Piliavin, 1972; Albrecht *et al.*, 1982).

The effect of disability on self-image, however, is more complex than simply being negative. Zeldow and Pavlou's (1984) study of predominantly female multiple sclerosis patients found that the severity of the illness rather than its duration was important in determining self-concept. While women with multiple sclerosis may have poor feelings about their bodies, their self-image often remains intact. Other studies of severe disabling conditions have also not found women to be especially low on self-esteem (Knudson-Cooper 1981; Frank 1984; Gething 1985). Bonwich's (1985) study of women who had an injury to their spinal cord found them to have increased self-esteem as a result of having mastered demanding new roles and overcome formidable obstacles to do so. The injury had also provided the stimulus to free themselves from the constraints imposed by feminine sex role stereotypes. Therefore, despite disability and sometimes because of it, many women achieve a healthy and strong sense of self-worth. Sometimes, the challenge of the disability itself allows them to gain insights and develop capacities that they might otherwise not have done.

Many women with disabilities recognise how much their sexual lives contribute to feelings of self-worth and restoring a battered self-confidence, (Duffy, 1981, p. 49; Campling, 1981a, p. 42). However, this can coincide with a woman feeling that sex with her is not as good as it would be with someone who is not disabled. Much of this is due to the way in which a woman has been characterised in our society. It can also make a woman vulnerable to the attentions of men whose motives are exploitative and uncaring. A study of victims of sexual abuse in the United States found that women with disabilities were equally vulnerable to it as other women. However, almost all the sexual offenders were people well known to the victim, frequently care-givers or relatives (Ryerson, 1981). The psycho-logical consequences and the dynamics of the abuse may be no different to those experienced by other abused women. For a woman with a disability, however, there are additional problems. If the abuser is a care-giver or 'a relative upon whom she depends, reporting the abuse may mean a further loss of independence and possible institutionalisation where she cannot be guaranteed protection from further abuse.

Women who are disabled often feel themselves to be considered 'neutered sexual beings' where the issue at stake is one of establishing sexual eligibility in society (Shaul *et al.*, 1978; Bullard and Knight, 1981; Campling, 1981a). This does not necessarily mean such women having to adopt a traditional feminine role, but having their sexuality and their right to physical and emotional relationships without exploitation recognised. Duffy's study of seventy-seven women with a variety of disabilities concludes that they have been placed in a 'no-win' situation. By treating women in general as sexual playthings and yet women with disabilities as asexual, she suggests that 'Society has more or less successfully barred us from participation in the only sphere in which it has been deemed we might experience self worth' (Duffy, 1981, p.63). In an attempt to establish the principle that women who are disabled are not asexual, an Australian woman who is disabled recently posed for a men's magazine consisting of sexually titillating photographs. In establishing one principle, however, she could be said to have helped deny another, that women's sexuality is not typified by the stereotyped and commercialised portrayals found in semi-pornographic literature.

Sexuality is also publicly associated with a standard of attractiveness for both men and women. In men, the standard relates to power and wealth; in women it relates to physical appearance. In this area the effects of physical disablement on a woman can be very considerable. The experience of being placed outside the realm of possible sexual activity takes a number of forms in relation to women with disabilities. Assumptions are made that they do not have sexual feelings, that they will never get married or have a relationship that includes sex, and, by implication, that they will not have children. This attitude is manifested in the lack of information that there is for disabled women on sexual activity, contraception and childbirth. It is most clearly manifested in institutional settings where there is a lack of privacy, such as not having locks on doors, so that people are unable to give expression to their sexual feelings and needs.

Given the logistical problems which might arise from spasticity, incontinence, sensory or motor deficits and changes, it is likely that there is an even greater need for advice and information on sexual activity for people with disabilities. However, very little work has been done and almost no advice is available in traditional settings. The invisibility of women with disabilities as far as sexuality is concerned is noticeable, for example, in the field of spinal cord injuries. A large body of data exists on the sexual functioning of men mainly related to coitus, in contrast to a dearth of information on women (Thornton, 1981; Bonwich, 1985). Bonwich suggests that this is due to the view that women function sexually in a relatively passive manner. However, studies are increasingly being done which tell a very different story. Some have noted the extent to which women can experience orgasm and sexual pleasure despite the lack of sensation and motion in significant parts of their bodies (Bullard and Knight, 1981; Shaul *et al.*, 1978; Duffy, 1981; Campling, 1981a). There is also some evidence of women discovering new erogenous zones after disability, with heightened sensations in those parts of their body not affected by the disability (Mathews, 1983, p. 64) The experience of disability may result in women being forced to learn more about themselves sexually which can enhance their sex life. A woman with cerebral palsy, for instance, reports finding herself having to direct her partner explicitly before or during lovemaking, which increased the enjoyment for both of them (Bullard and Knight, 1981).

The possibility of having a relationship with someone depends in the first instance on having the social opportunities to meet people. If women are isolated at home or in institutions, unable to get jobs or into inaccessible buildings, they will immediately be limited in their circle of friends and acquaintances. It will not be their ability to perform sexually that determines their relationships, but the attitudes of others and the opportunities available to them. Ironically, women with disabilities can simultaneously experience social isolation and invasion of privacy. Privacy very often flies out the window for the woman who becomes disabled. Her body becomes available to other people – to parents, to doctors, to nurses, to physiotherapists, and to groups of medical students on ward rounds. At the same time as everything around her tells her that women keep their bodies covered in public, that women's bodies are uncovered only for sexual purposes, she often feels her body to be flaunted and used, peered and poked at, subtly being told that she is asexual – yet another variation on the theme of ambiguity which has always surrounded women and their bodies. A number of women have written and spoken about their deep sense of affront and humiliation, and even of violation at being prodded and poked by a succession of professionals. It seems to be very rare that women in this position are given any sense of control over events, even by being asked for their permission to be prodded and poked.

Once a woman is in a relationship, she may confront the dilemma of birth control. However, regulation of fertility for women with disabilities is another facet of sexuality that has been badly neglected. Women with physical disabilities do not seem to face the same pressures to be sterilised as some women with intellectual disabilities (Duffy, 1981, p. 123), although there is evidence of abortions being inappropriately offered to them (Bullard and Knight, 1981, p. 71; Campling, 1981a, p. 91). This may be because of the fear that they will be unable to cope with caring for a child and that other members of the family or the state will have to assume parental responsibility. The number of women who have children, love them and care for them well, regardless of their disabilities, suggests that this belief is unfounded. The problems attached to being a mother who is disabled have less to do with neglect of the child than with society's neglect of the mother. Having a baby is expensive; requiring special or appropriate equipment makes it even more so. Being a mother can be isolating and exhausting as well as rewarding. A woman who is disabled may need additional help and assistance at various times (National Childbirth Trust, 1984). However, as with sexuality, many women with disabilities show considerable inventiveness in constructing appropriate ways of expressing themselves and handling the situations with which they are confronted (Duffy, 1981; Mathews, 1983; NCT, 1984).

The image of ideal 'womanhood' extends beyond physical appearance to lifestyle. During their lifetimes, women are expected to fulfil a number of roles. These include being lovers, mothers providing and rearing the next generation, housewives or home-makers providing sustenance and care for working men, carers, and potential members of the paid workforce available for that part of the economy if it needs them. Women who live out this model find that it materially disadvantages them (Lonsdale, 1987). Women who are denied or unable or do not wish to fill these roles are stigmatised and face possible rejection. Whereas some feminists may choose to opt out of such roles, other women who have deviated from them (such as career women by choice or women with disabilities by chance) may find themselves pursuing markedly feminine roles in an attempt to redeem themselves and regain some value (Saxton,1981). When women with disabilities do decide to opt out as feminists, it is often not recognised as a positive choice (Campling, 1981a).

The present study

The message that seems to be emerging from a number of studies is that our society makes certain demands on women which are difficult and stressful for many women to meet, especially those with physical disabilities. The aim of this book is to explore this by considering the effects of physical disablement on women. This will be done by a general discussion of the social context of disability, including a review of the history of disability policy. This is preceded by a review of some recent evidence regarding the prevalence of disability with particular reference to women. Thereafter, the book will generally review and discuss a number of studies in five main areas, drawing on the interviews undertaken.

First, the book considers the way in which women with disabilities have been rendered invisible by a society which makes inadequate provision for their requirements, and is discomforted and inconvenienced by their presence.

Second, it looks at the importance and significance of physical disability on a women's self-image and her body image. The women who were interviewed are asked about their experiences of sexuality, relationships, marriage, and child-rearing, all of which not only contribute towards the kind of self-image women have of themselves, but also reflect the attitudes and behaviour of others towards them.

Thirdly, the book considers the extent to which physical disability makes someone dependent, financially and psychologically. Dependency has particular implications for women because of the important part which gender plays in determining whether someone is expected or encouraged, or indeed is even allowed to be independent. Since women are encouraged to play a mcre dependent role in society than men, women with disabilities often have a particular struggle to achieve control over their own destinies, although they are sometimes 'allowed' out of the passive and dependent female role.

Dependency is often manifested in material poverty and a loss or lack of income. Fourth, therefore, the extent to which physical disability predisposes someone towards poverty is considered. The particular pattern of disadvantage experienced by women with disabilities is outlined within two of the major distributive systems that affect them, employment and social security. Key social policies directed at these two systems are analysed.

Finally, the book looks at the extent to which women who are or become physically disabled experience discrimination and a loss of civil liberties.

The book concludes by considering the ways in which women with disabilities achieve greater independence and self-determination, and the policies which assist or hinder them. It concludes that there has been little opportunity for self-determination by women with disabilities. They are constrained by sex role stereotypes of women and by professional ideas of what services they need. Recently, this has begun to change with the political organisation of people with disabilities who are redefining the problem and creating alternative service structures. These include the formation of pressure groups (Ablon, 1981; Oliver, 1984), the establishment of assertiveness training groups (Kolb, 1981) and of peer counselling programmes (Saxton, 1981; Burgess, 1985; Derbyshire Coalition of Disabled People, 1985). Perhaps most significant has been the establishment of Centres for Independent and Integrated Living, which attempt to ensure that a wide range of services are derived from the direct experience of people who are themselves disabled.

Women with disabilities are not a homogeneous group. They range across different ages, educational backgrounds, and socio-economic classes. They have a variety of personal circumstances and may experience a mild or a severe disability. The two things they do have in common are their gender and the fact of their physical disablement. Different impairments have differing disabling effects, but most people with a disability are handicapped primarily in the range of choices available to them – where to live, what sort of educational opportunities are around, what employment is on offer, and what sort of leisure or social activities are available to them. These primary handicapping conditions often lead on to secondary handicaps such as lack of access to material resources and the experience of poverty.

A number of women were interviewed for this book who had a range of different physical disabilities which they all felt had led to them being handicapped by others and by the social institutions with which they came into contact. The women who were interviewed were not intended to be representative but to encompass a range of women of different ages, races and backgrounds who experienced a number of different disabilities. They ranged in age from nineteen to fifty-seven years old. Their mean age was thirty-seven years. Elderly women were not included because the study aimed to find out about attempts to live independently, to work, to obtain an income, and to participate in the ordinary life of the community. Age is a factor which influences all these things in its own right.

Seventeen of the women interviewed were white, three were Asian, and two were Afro-Carribean. Their disabilities spanned sensory impairments, diseases such as multiple sclerosis, polio, arthritis and muscular dystrophy, spinal cord injuries, and congenital conditions such as cerebral palsy. Nine of the women were single, ten were either married or living with a partner, and three were widowed or divorced. Ten women had children. Eleven women were in paid employment, two were self-employed, eight were unemployed, and one worked in a voluntary capacity. Only one woman lived in local authority residential care. The remainder lived either in their own homes (sixteen) or in council accommodation (five).

In addition to talking about their experience of various social policies, the women also spoke about their ability to lead ordinary lives and the attitudes of other people towards them. They spoke too about employment, their material resources and discrimination. In analysing what they said, an attempt was made to look at their experiences not only in terms of a personal history but rather in terms of the effect that social and economic forces have on the outcome of physical difference.

2

The prevalence of disability

The prevalence of disability in any society depends on the way it has been defined and measured. Some definitions have emerged from discussions which are primarily conceptual and theoretical (World Health Organisation, 1980; Agerholm, 1975a, 1975b). Others have been devised with a practical purpose in mind such as surveys to count and classify people (Harris 1971; Martin *et al.*, 1988) or for allocating benefits and services (OUTSET, 1986a, 1986b). Some writers have tried to develop both types of definition (Townsend, 1979). Attempts to measure and classify individual impairments and disabilities have been made for purposes of providing material relief since the days of the Poor Law and workmen's compensation since the nineteenth century (Brown, 1982, 1984). In recent years these attempts have become more sophisticated, incorporating not only a medical or physiological view of disability but also a social and political view of the phenomenon of disability which emphasises the interaction between environmental and social processes and health states (see Duckworth, 1983, p. 16, for a review of these developments).

The latter approach has been more concerned with the outcome or consequences of disease and impairment than with the health state itself. A good example of this is the International Classification of Impairments, Disabilities and Handicaps (ICIDH), first published by the World Health Organisation in 1980. Based on work done at Manchester University by Wood and his colleagues, it proposed a classification system relating to the consequences of disease, disorder or injury. The system is concerned to identify not only intrinsic health states or deviations from a biomedical norm, but the process that ensues from the onset of disease, injury or disorder to the final experience of being handicapped which incorporates social disadvantage. An illustration of the process an individual may undergo might be the following. Due to injury or disease, an individual may develop a skeletal or aural *impairment*. This may lead respectively to a *disability* in locomotion or communication. The person may then be *handicapped* on a number of dimensions such as physical independence, social integration, economic self-sufficiency or choice of occupation.

The importance of the ICIDH system is that it does not classify or label people but states of health in the broadest sense. It advocates describing people as 'having' a disability rather than 'being' disabled, which is seen to be stigmatising and disadvantageous. It is also concerned to extend the notion of disability to include the social and environmental forces that create handicap and to outline the process of social disadvantage that can ensue from disease, disorder or injury. It provides a more precise terminology for describing certain behaviours and circumstances. Duckworth suggests that the scheme has practical uses, for example in screening people for school or job placements or for rehousing people more appropriately because it can 'determine both a profile of the individual's functional abilities and a reciprocal specification of the environment with the intention of identifying discrepancies' (Duckworth, 1983, p. 100). In practice, however, most countries are still very far from such a comprehensive view of disability.

In determining eligibility for social security benefits or for various services such as participation in employment schemes or the provision of aids and housing adaptations, administrative procedures are usually used to standardise the criteria used. Medical opinion is usually the determining factor of eligibility underlying many of these procedures, particularly with regard to social security. Medical certification, for instance, is required in claiming most disability benefits in both the United Kingdom and the United States. A medical test or examination is considered to be an objective way of determining eligibility for various services or cash payments in both countries. This applies regardless of whether the cash payment is claimed on the basis of social insurance, such as Invalidity Benefit in the UK and Disability Insurance in the USA, or means testing. Consequently, a medical approach to disability prevails which not only focuses on anatomical or physiological loss or abnormality, but implies that disability is a phenomenon that can only be revealed and understood through the clinical approach of medical practitioners. As Stone (1984) points out, this means that 'doctors preside over an enormous income transfer program'.

This was exemplified in the war and industrial pension schemes developed earlier this century, as well as the more recent severe disablement allowance (SDA) in Britain, where the loss of a faculty or bodily organ plays a key role in determining whether and how much a person gets by way of compensation. These can be very precise judgements. In Britain, for instance, the loss of one eye without complications is judged to represent a 40 per cent degree of disablement, the loss of an index finger 14 per cent, while an amputation below the shoulder with a stump 'less than 20.5 centimetres from tip of acromion' represents an 80 per cent degree of disablement. Such practices are used in social security systems throughout the world, although there are considerable variations in the scales used for the same impairment (Walker, 1981). The importance placed on such clinical precision makes it difficult to incorporate other types of judgement about the extent to which someone is handicapped by their disability. Even in situations when medical adjudication is reviewed, the issue is often not so much about lay versus medical involvement but about whether the examining doctor should be the individual's own general practitioner or an officially designated medical officer (Oglesby, 1983).

The limitation of this medical approach to assessing disability is that it does not accurately measure the extent to which a person can or cannot perform certain functions. It also tends to be oriented towards physical rather than mental processes, and towards the individual rather than the social context in which a task must be performed. The physical orientation is undoubtedly partly due to the origins of such assessment schemes, which were formulated to assess injuries arising out of war or industrial production. But it has had the unintended effect of excluding or ignoring people whose disabilities may have had their origins elsewhere, such as women, who are less involved in wars and industrial production. It also reflects the status of the medical profession which, in advanced industrial societies, has been granted powers of regulation and sanction in certain areas. Their involvement in the assessment of disability has led to a narrow conception of what disability means.

Adopting this model for use in social security systems such as in the severe disablement allowance scheme in Britain, is likely to have serious consequences for the many female recipients of SDA, an issue which will be considered in greater depth in Chapter 8.

In attempting to overcome these limitations, a form of assessment based on functional loss and restriction of activities has been developed and proposed as an alternative way of defining and measuring disability. This was the approach adopted by the first national survey of disability undertaken in Britain in 1968, in which impairment was defined as lacking part or all of a limb, or having a defective limb, organ or mechanism of the body; disablement as the loss or reduction of functional ability; and handicap as the disadvantage or restriction of activity caused by disability, (Harris, 1971, p. 2) In practice, disability was defined in terms of the individual's performance in undertaking self-care activities such as bathing, feeding and dressing themselves. Again the focus was on physical activity. The social dimensions of the ability to perform self-care were not reflected, although the approach was a significant improvement on the crude percentage assessment of disability based on loss of faculty.

Many independent surveys undertaken by academic researchers engaged in the study of disability, who wished to devise better methods of determining the true numbers of people with disabilities have used similar tests of functional incapacity (Townsend, 1979; Sainsbury, 1973; Jeffreys *et al.*, 1969). According to Townsend, who has also been concerned with the application of definitions to policy, there are at least five different meanings in the term 'disability'. These are disability as anatomical, physiological or psychological abnormality or loss; as a chronic clinical condition altering or interrupting the physiological or psychological process;· as a functional limitation on ordinary activity; as socially deviant behaviour; and as a socially defined class and status. He operationalises two of these concepts, impairment and functional incapacity, to provide two measures of disability which can be used for survey purposes. He recognises the limitations of using only selected activities which are not weighted and the inability of such measures to take into account daily or seasonal fluctuations in ability. However, in the context of the survey, he sees functional measures as preferable to those social measures which are incomplete or quixotic (Townsend, 1979, pp. 686–93).

Walker (1981) suggests that it is possible to assess severity of incapacity for the purposes of administering benefits and services on the basis of a social conception of disability. He attempts to construct an index for this purpose and finds that it achieves a reasonable level of agreement with medical assessments. While the assessment suggested is primarily based on the functional limitations which an impairment places on an individual, the functions measured include the performance of not only physical tasks but also social roles and obligations. Consequently, the assessment is divided into three areas of activity: capacity for self-care and household management, the capacity for social communication and participation, and the capacity for employment. Walker recognises that the components of such an index will depend on social conventions. This is particularly so for measurements of social communication and participation, but will also apply to the other two areas.

The rationale for broadening the definition and measurement of disability is to arrive at a multi-dimensional concept which incorporates as many elements of a person's life as possible. This is to ensure that all an individual's needs as well as different individual needs are potentially able to be met when that definition is put to a practical purpose. It is also to ensure that in the provision of benefits and services, some individuals are not left out due to the particular limitations they might experience. In recent years this has led to increasing calls for a greater involvement of the person being assessed in the whole process of assessment. One approach to ascertaining the prevalence of disability has been to screen whole populations, allowing individuals to assess themselves as disabled or not. This is based on the philosophy that people with disabilities are the best qualified to talk about their lives and needs (OUTSET, 1987b). Another approach has been to put forward a set of principles and procedures for developing an improved form of assessment which takes self-assessment as an essential starting point but which also incorporates other forms of functional assessment (Disability Alliance, 1987, pp. 37–42).

The variety of definitions and survey techniques used have led to varying estimates of the size of the population with a disability (see Table 2.1). According to the first national survey of disability in Britain, there were just over one million individuals who were very severely, severely, or appreciably handicapped according to a set of criteria involving self-care (Harris, 1971). The survey was restricted to people over the age of sixteen living in private households. An independent survey undertaken at the same time, however, found that three times as many people over the age of ten years were severely or appreciably incapacitated, although this was reduced to twice as many when those not specifying their disabling condition were removed (Townsend, 1979, p. 696). A more recent survey in 1983 estimated, on the basis of five area surveys, that the handicapped population in the United Kingdom was over two million, which was considerably higher than the total contained in all local Social Services registers for the same period (OUTSET, 1983). This meant that by 1983, estimates of this population ranged from about 3 to 6 per cent. None of these surveys included people living in hospitals or residential homes. This suggests, therefore, that all were underestimating the size of the population.

Table 2.1   *Different estimates of the prevalence of disability prior to 1988*

	Number
OPCS, 1968 (GB)	1,128,000
Townsend, 1968 (UK)	3,095,000
Townsend, 1968 (UK)	1,935,000
Outset, 1983 (UK)	2,065,926
Social Services Register, 1982–3 (UK)	1,333,494

Haveman *et al.* (1984) have compared the incidence of disability in the working age population of eight industrialised countries, as shown in Table 2.2. The two countries with the lowest incidence were France and the UK, with 3.4 and 3.6 per cent respectively. According to the authors, the statistical basis for collecting information in these two countries was very weak, suggesting an underestimate which subsequent surveys have confirmed. The two countries with the highest incidence were Sweden and the USA, with 17.7 and 14.6 per cent respectively. In these two countries, the collection of data was the most accurate, although the figures exaggerate the incidence by including people who were not permanently disabled.

Table 2.2   *Incidence of disability in the working age*
population in selected countries (1978)

Country	Percentage
Federal Republic of Germany	7.3
France	3.4
Israel	4.5
Italy	9.3
The Netherlands	8.2
Sweden	17.7
United Kingdom	3.6
United States	14.6
Canada	9.2

Source: Robert H. Haveman *et al.* (1984) *Public Policy towards Disabled Workers*, Cornell University Press, Table 2.2. *Report of the Canadian health and disability survey*, 1983–84, Table 1.

The source of these data is in the main from surveys based on self-reported health status. Although there are always limitations to these kinds of comparative data, they provide a useful basis for comparison. However, they also reflect differences in the way in which disability has been defined and measured. The figure for the United Kingdom needs to be revised due to more recent survey data.

In Britain in 1988 a new set of national estimates were published by the Office of Population Censuses and Surveys (OPCS) based on four national surveys undertaken between 1985 and 1988. These surveys will be examined in some detail, as they constituted a new departure in the measurement of disability. They were far more extensive than the earlier survey in that they covered people with all types of disability – physical, sensory and mental. Planned in three stages, they also included children and people in institutions. In an attempt to meet the criticism of the earlier survey that many people were excluded because they did not respond to the questionnaire, an additional effort was made to pursue a sample of those people not responding initially. The surveys constructed a new measure of disability based on the view that it is misleading to see people as

either disabled or non-disabled. Instead, disability was conceptualised as a continuum ranging from very severe to slight disability.
Taking this view means that the extent of disability will depend
upon at what point on the continuum a threshold is set above which
people are defined as disabled. The authors of the study stress that
there is no absolute prevalence of disability, as rates of disability
depend on how it has been defined and measured.

The importance of this approach is that it moves away from the
simplistic dichotomy between disablement and nondisablement that
is implicit in the allocation of most disability benefits, which ignore
or deny the possibility of partial incapacity. Instead it moves
towards recognising the importance of the severity of disability as
well as the complex nature of many disabling conditions which are
not fixed or steady (Martin *et al.*, 1988).

The study adopts the definitions of disablement proposed in the
World Health Organisation's International Classification of
Impairments, Disabilities and Handicaps, which, as mentioned
earlier, identifies three different concepts which are consequent upon
disease (shown in Figure 2.1).

Figure 2.1

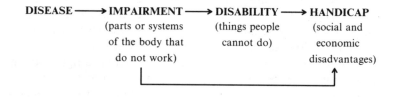

The definition includes a sociological dimension, therefore implicitly
seeing disablement as more than simply an individual problem.
Impairment, disability and handicap are defined as conceptually
different, with different implications with regard to strategies of
intervention, say, in policy terms. The focus of the survey, however,
is on measuring 'disability' or the things people can and cannot do.
Its prevalence rates were based on this, although information was
also collected on handicaps in order to investigate the extent to
which disability results in handicap. Inevitably the measure of
disability arrived at faces the same difficulties of how to incorporate
a social dimension which not only includes disability in social

functioning but also the magnitude of disadvantage experienced. The study is concerned with measuring 'disability' because it was commissioned to provide up-to-date information on the numbers of disabled people in Britain for the purposes of planning benefits and services. Consequently, it collected information about people's limitations in doing certain things and then used a novel procedure for combining information about different disabilities in order to reach an overall measure of severity of disability for each person.

This was done by having approximately 100 people make judgements to assess the level of severity of certain limitations within ten main areas of potential disability: locomotion, reaching and stretching, dexterity, seeing, hearing, personal care, continence, communication, behaviour, intellectual functioning. (Three more were added later: consciousness, eating, drinking and digestion, and disfigurement.) Thus, for instance, in the area of locomotion they were asked to rate in order of seriousness various aspects of mobility such as 'cannot walk at all', 'has fallen 12 or more times in the last year', 'cannot walk 50 yards (or 200 or 400 yards) without stopping or severe discomfort', and so on.

The judgements were carried out between disabilities within the ten areas, between the ten areas, and between different combinations of disability. The criteria of overall severity was based on a consensus of assessments by the judges. The judges included people working in the field of disability as well as people with disabilities themselves.

On this basis national estimates were made of the extent of disability at various levels of severity in late 1980s Britain, and these were higher estimates than found in any previous study. However, as the authors are careful to point out, this does not imply an increase in rates of disability over the intervening nineteen years, but rather a difference in the way disability was measured in the later survey. Therefore the increase may be due to the use of a relatively low threshold of disability, or to the more sophisticated techniques of measurement devised.

The report of the survey illustrates the kind of person who would have been included in the count at various levels of severity. For instance, two examples given of people who were considered so mildly disabled that they fell into categories 1 and 2 respectively were (a) a man who was deaf in one ear, which meant that he had difficulty hearing someone talk in a normal voice in a quiet room, and (b) a woman with angina and an eye problem which meant that she could not walk 200 yards without stopping or severe discomfort, nor could she see well enough to recognise a friend across the road and had difficulty reading ordinary newspaper print (Martin *et al.*, 1988, p. 13). Considering these two illustrative case studies, the threshold used does not seem unduly low. Its importance, however, is in giving some indication of future need. People at the lower thresholds of disability today are undoubtedly the more severely disabled people of tomorrow.

The total number of adults found to be disabled was 6,202,000, of whom 422,000 lived in communal establishments and 5,780,000 in private households. As would be expected, there were fewer people in the higher severity categories in private households, but the reverse was true for communal establishments, as Table 2.3 illustrates.

Table 2.3   *Proportions of disabled adults in Great Britain (1988) (percentages)*

Level of severity	Total	Private households	Communal estab.
Category 10 (most severe)	3.4	1.8	25.6
9	5.9	4.9	18.9
8	6.4	5.8	13.7
7	7.8	7.7	9.2
6	8.8	8.8	8.0
5	11.4	11.7	6.9
4	11.3	11.7	6.3
3	12.1	12.7	4.5
2	13.5	14.2	3.8
Category 1 (least severe)	19.3	20.5	3.0

Source: Martin *et al.* (1988) *The prevalence of disability among adults*, calculated from Table 3.1.

In western industrial societies there has been an increase in chronic and disabling diseases which have replaced traumatic injuries and infectious diseases as major causes of disablement. Despite this, there is still a tendency to regard disabled people as young and confined to wheelchairs as a result of polio, paraplegia or amputation, and policies are still developed as if this were so (Bury, 1979). The most prominent example of this stereotype was the logo used for the United Nations International Year of Disabled People in 1981 (see below). This is still the international symbol used to indicate most public facilities for people with disabilities and in many publications on disability, particularly those of United Nations organisations. The reality is very different, of course, with only about one in ten disabled adults having not yet reached middle age, and the causes of severe disability being predominantly arthritis, problems of the nervous system such as strokes and Parkinson's disease, and mental disabilities. The dominant image of disability, therefore, is a partial one which does not take sufficiently into account factors such as age, sex and the underlying causes of the disability.

Table 2.4   *Percentage of complaints causing disability among adults in Great Britain (1988)*

Classification of complaints	Private households	Communal estab.
Musculo-skeletal	46	37
Ear complaints	38	13
Eye complaints	22	17
Circulatory system	20	16
Respiratory system	13	6
Nervous system	13	30
Mental problems	13	50
Digestive system	6	10
Genito-urinary	3	10
Endocrine, metabolic	2	8
Neoplasm	2	4
Skin diseases	1	2
Blood disorders	1	2
Infection	1	0
Other	6	10

Note: The percentages do not add up to 100 as some people had more than one complaint.

Source: Martin *et al.* (1988) *The Prevalence of Disability among Adults*, extracted from Table 4.3.

In the OPCS study, the medical conditions or impairments causing disability varied. Table 2.4 shows the OPCS findings (according to a modified version of the International Classification of Diseases).

The main causes of severe disability among people living in both private households and communal establishments are musculo-skeletal complaints, of which arthritis is predominant. This is followed by diseases of the nervous system including strokes, Parkinson's disease and multiple sclerosis in communal establishments, and deafness and blindness in private households.

Often a higher rate of disability can be found in black populations than white populations, although this can vary in different communities and between different ethnic groups. In Britain there is a higher rate of adult disability among Afro-Carribean households, where the rate is 151 per thousand adults as against 137 per thousand in white households and 126 per thousand in Asian households (standardised to take account of the different age profiles of each of these groups). The reasons for this are not clear. It may be due to patterns of social and economic disadvantage experienced and the different types of jobs undertaken, as well as specific health problems affecting the Afro-Carribean population such as thessalemia and sickle cell anaemia. In the USA, the incidence of severe disablement among working-age adults is 7.9 per cent for whites and 12.3 per cent for ethnic minorities (Havemen *et al.*, 1984) The composition of the population with disabilities is heavily weighted towards individuals with low educational attainment. Disability may therefore reflect, the combined effect of racial discrimination leading to poor schooling, employment in more hazardous unskilled jobs, and poor housing in less healthy environments.

Women

When we talk of physical disability in the late twentieth century, we are referring to an issue that is more likely to confront women than men. By a number of different measures, more women than men are likely to experience physical disability or a limiting long-standing illness. Although, from birth onwards, male mortality overall is higher than female mortality, the pattern is reversed with regard to female morbidity. Part of this is due to the longer life expectancy of women, which has been increasing in recent years relative to that of men. For example, in 1950 women could expect to live five years longer than men. By the 1980s they could expect to live 6.4 years longer than men (Central Statistical Office, 1986).

There are considerably more disabled women than men at all levels of severity except the lowest. There are 3,656,000 disabled women compared to 2,544,000 disabled men in Britain, the majority of whom have a physical disability. In particular, among the older age groups, women outnumber men substantially. There are almost one and a half million women over the age of 74 who are disabled, compared to 627,000 men over this age. This is only partly due to the greater longevity of women, as the prevalence rates among those over 74 are consistently higher for women than for men. Allowing for the different numbers of men and women over the age of 74, the rate of disability for women is still higher than it is for men, i.e. 63 per cent as against 53 per cent, indicating that elderly women are more likely to be disabled than elderly men. Not only are there higher proportions of disabled women than men in total over the age of 74, but this is true at each level of severity. The increase in the proportion of people over the age of 74 who are severely disabled is much steeper for women than it is for men.

There are differences between Britain and the USA with regard to the prevalence of disability among working-age women and men. In the USA, 8.5 per cent of all working age women compared with 9.5 per cent of all working-age men have a disability (Bowe, 1983). This changes if severity is taken into account, as 12.3 per cent of working-age women are severely disabled compared with only 7.9 per cent of all working-age men, (Haveman *et al.*, 1984) In Britain, 9 per cent of all working-age women compared with 8 per cent of all working-age men have a disability. This difference becomes exacerbated if severity is taken into account (Martin *et al.*, 1988, p. 22). In both countries, therefore, a higher proportion of women than men of working age are severely disabled. This does not apply in the case of children, at least in Britain. Girls up to the age of fifteen have a lower incidence of disability at all ages and at all severity levels. The increased prevalence of disability for women only begins to exceed that for men after the age of twenty (Bone and Meltzer, 1989, p. 21).

In total, the prevalence of disability in Britain is 142 per 1,000 people, but this changes dramatically at different age groups and between men and women, as has been indicated. Table 2.5 gives the prevalence rates according to age and sex.

Table 2.5   *The prevalence of disability according to age and sex (1988) (per thousand of the population)*

Age	Boys/men	Girls/women
0 - 15	37	26
16 - 59	56	64
60 - 74	283	264
75 and over	533	631
Total 16 +	121	161

Sources: Bone and Meltzer (1989) *The Prevalence of Disability among Children* Table 3.6. Martin *et al.* (1988) *The Prevalence of Disability among Adults*, extracted from Table 3.7.

Men tend to have an overall higher prevalence rate in one particular age band, namely between the ages of 60 and 64 if the lowest severity category 1 is included. Men of this age were more likely than women to report health problems or disabilities which were sufficient to include them in the lowest category of severity but not at higher levels of severity. The fact that these are the years preceding retirement for men was thought to be significant in causing this difference (Martin *et al.*, 1988, p. 24).

Differences in the prevalence rates are also more apparent for the total population than for those living in private households, reflecting the relatively large numbers of very elderly disabled women living in communal establishments. Fifty-eight per cent of people with disabilities in private households are women, as against 69 per cent in communal establishments. The vast majority of residents in communal establishments are elderly: two-thirds are over 74 and over a half are aged 80 or more. Although in absolute terms there are not more younger disabled men than women living in communal establishments, there is a higher proportion, i.e. 32 per cent of men living in such establishments are between 16 and 59 years of age as against only 10 per cent of women of that age. By contrast, only 44 per cent of men were over 74, compared to 77 per cent of women in communal establishments.

The frequency of impairment and disability at different levels of severity is important for a number of different reasons. It is necessary to know the incidence of chronic or severe disability in order to establish services and benefit systems which are appropriate to the requirements of people so disabled. The incidence of mild disability is equally important as an indicator of future requirements in service and benefit provision. What is increasingly becoming recognized as important are the different requirements of different groups of people with disabilities. What the following chapters will attempt to show are the particular experiences and needs of women who are physically disabled. There is growing evidence that many of their specific requirements as women have been either ignored or simply not seen. Given the greater incidence of disability generally among women, such neglect can be said to require redress.

3

The social context of disability

The roots of modern forms of state support and provision for people with disabilities are to be found in the nineteenth-century Poor Law. Apart from injunctions by the Church to be charitable, a minimalist form of state provision emerged in Britain out of the Poor Law. Along with people who were sick, in need and elderly, people with disabilities were eligible for some financial support in the form of outdoor relief. For those whose disabilities were particularly severe there was also the possibility of institutional care in the workhouse, i.e. indoor relief. To some extent, people with disabilities may have been treated less harshly in being more likely to be subject to outdoor relief than to the dreaded workhouse, in that the workhouse was an attempt to deter the able-bodied poor who refused to take up paid employment. The intention of Poor Law policy was that outdoor relief should be the main form of assistance given to people who were sick or disabled. But if their sickness or disability became prolonged, the recipients of outdoor relief would experience strong pressure to enter the workhouse (Brown, 1984, p. 2). The reason for this can be found in the underlying philosophy of the Poor Law, which was that of deterrence. This meant that people had to be discouraged from trying to get something for nothing and had to be induced as far as possible to obtain an income by their own means, namely by selling their labour.

The harshest application of the policy of deterrence was to be found among the able-bodied poor, who could usually only get poor relief if they were prepared to enter the workhouse. There, the austere and oppressive conditions would ensure that only those people whose need was desperate and absolute would claim poor relief. The provision of such relief also generated the stigma of not being capable of earning a living, as well as the stigma of possibly being someone who was deliberately evading employment. The work ethic which determined these policies, as well as being fostered by them in turn, was convenient and useful to the owners of factories every hungry for labour to work their capital profitably.

A large proportion of the recipients of outdoor relief were people who were either chronically sick or disabled and who were therefore acknowledged to be more deserving of help. However, the Poor Law administrators were concerned that if a better and more amenable system was provided for some recipients such as those who were chronically sick and disabled, then this would pave the way for people pretending to be ill. Consequently, people who were chronically sick or disabled were often admitted to the workhouse, either on suspicion of malingering or more benignly, as a form of asylum for those people whose disabilities were more profound. Once in the workhouse, however, the malign or benign distinction was likely to become blurred, with most poor people with disabilities bearing a burden of blame and guilt for their individual condition. One can readily imagine that certain forms of disability may have attracted harsher treatment, such as the less visible diseases or disabilities such as arthritis, deafness and so on, especially in their early stages.

In addition to this, chronically sick or disabled people who were felt to need some kind of medical or supervisory care, were likely to find themselves in a Poor Law infirmary. They may not have had their labour exacted from them as they would have done in a workhouse, but as they were unlikely to leave the asylum, it often became the place in which they would go to die. There were frequent scandals about the treatment of poorer people who were sick, despite the fact that the infirmary was intended to be a 'soft option' to the workhouse. The Metropolitan Poor Law Act and the Poor Law Ammendment Act were designed to ensure that sick and disabled people went into asylums rather than workhouses. What tended to happen, however, was that those who were chronically ill continued to be placed in workhouses, whereas those who were acutely ill went into hospitals (Brown, 1984, p. 3). Ironically, not only were different classes of ill and disabled people created, but the more severely ill or disabled a person was, the more they tended to be penalised. At times, this was extended to the families of disabled people, who had to follow them into the workhouse. One can surmise that this must have created an incentive for husbands and wives to desert their disabled partners.

A number of the individual conditions leading to disability were created by the appalling circumstances in which many people lived and worked. Early industrialisation is synonymous with hard and brutalised labour, low wages and poor housing, to say nothing of the conditions of much factory work, which was dangerous to health and safety. Many adult paupers were disabled as a consequence of their lives as child paupers:

> Pauper children shipped north from London workhouses in order to save ratepayers the cost of their maintenance were particularly unprotected. From the age of seven, children in factories had to work twelve to fifteen hours a day (or night), six days a week 'at best in monotonous toil, at worst in a hell of human cruelty'. The tale never ended of fingers cut off and limbs crushed in the wheels. (Hill, 1969, p. 264)

The reason these conditions continued as long as they did was in part due to a general belief in the dangers of idleness and the equation of idleness with sin by the Church. Again, such a belief was opportune for employers, as it would encourage a ready supply of labour without a necessarily accompanying concern about the conditions under which those labourers worked. The poor were considered to require 'regulation' for their spiritual health, and rights were thought to foster idleness (Tawney, 1926, p. 257).

Women and children were just as vulnerable to disabling accidents at work and to the dangers of disease, given the poor state of public health. But they were especially vulnerable to the workhouse. In a memorandum to the Boards of Poor Law Guardians in 1878, outdoor relief was expressly proscribed for certain categories of women, i.e. single able-bodied women with or without children, able-bodied widows with children except in some circumstances, and women deserted by their husbands (Thane, 1982, p. 306). Although the focus was on able-bodied women, it is interesting to note that the restriction on deserted women did not specify such a status. If desertion of women by their husbands when they became disabled was as prevalent then as it allegedly is today (see Chapter 5), then the intention of the Poor Law Guardians seems to have been for such women to go into the workhouse along with their able-bodies sisters.

Alongside the system of punitive state provision was the expansion of charitable agencies during the nineteenth century, including the large and influential Charity Organisation Society (COS). While some charities offered protection against the harshness of the Poor Law, the tension between religious and moral imperatives to help individuals on the one hand, and secular obligations on the other, was not very great. The disapproval of idleness by the Church has already been mentioned. Tawney has also shown how the Church and the state acted together in coping with pauperism, moral and social obligations often being seen as one, especially in the early days of the Poor Law (Tawney, 1926, pp 155–79). Later in the nineteenth century, the charitable organisations entered into this alliance. The largest single inspiration to charitable effort was religion. Three-quarters of the voluntary charities established in the second half of the nineteenth century were evangelical in origin (Thane, 1982, p. 20). Aside from their families, therefore, indigent people who became disabled had the same recourse as anyone else to the state, the Church and the charities if they needed help.

The Charity Organisation Society tried to co-ordinate most of the charities. In many respects its attitudes were not dissimilar to those of the Poor Law. It supported moves to replace the financial support of outdoor relief by an individualistic mode of help known as case-work, the precursor to modern day social work, and tried to encourage sick clubs and friendly societies as forms of self-help (Brown, 1984, p. 4; Thane, 1982, p. 22). Because of the exacting and stigmatising nature of the workhouse, the case-work offered by the COS may have been welcome as a more benevolent form of help. But it was as unequivocal as the Poor Law that the problem of poverty and its solution lay within the will of the individual. The replacement of outdoor relief with case-work made this even clearer.

Friendly societies grew steadily as an alternative form of financial self-help. By offering a weekly benefit or sum of money to their members in times of sickness, the friendly societies often enabled someone to avoid the reaches of the Poor Law and the workhouse. However, this support was generally only useful for short-term sickness and could not cope with long-term or lifelong disability.

Although by the end of the nineteenth century a large proportion of working men were members of one of these societies, membership was concentrated among skilled male workers, and many excluded women as members. Where women were allowed membership, they often became ineligible if they left the labour market, as women often did, to marry or have children (Brown, 1984, p. 4). It may be that women were less likely to become members both because of their lesser eligibility and because of expectations within families that they would play a lesser and more dependent role. Whatever the reason, their lower membership made them more vulnerable to the Poor Law option or to no help at all. The more fragile attachment that women with disabilities had to the labour market meant that they were even less likely to have recourse to this kind of help and even more likely to face the workhouse.

Poverty and disability, for both women and men, were inextricably linked. In many cases, poverty caused disability in that low paid or manual workers were more vulnerable to accident and disease. Poor housing and the environmental pollution that particularly afflicted poor districts increased the likelihood of accidents in the home and created diseases. Once disabled, the downward spiral into even greater poverty proceeded apace, with most avenues to employment closed off and only a meagre and reluctant form of poor relief available. In as much as both the moral and secular response to poverty tried to control the behaviour of the poor, so too did it try to control the lives and behaviour of those who were disabled.

How have circumstances changed for people, and especially women, with disabilities? Clearly, it would be foolish to suggest that they had not. The conditions of industrial production have improved due to technological advances as well as the promulgation of a number of laws and policies regulating the health and safety of the working environment: nutrition has improved, housing has become better, infectious diseases have declined, and a welfare state has replaced the Poor Law. The specifics of life and work have changed, even if certain fundamental beliefs have not.

Accompanying these changes, however, have come an increase in stress-related diseases, chronic and degenerative conditions of the circulatory and respiratory systems, and various cancers. As people live longer due to advances in medical science, so they become more vulnerable to conditions such as these. Since women constitute a far higher proportion of the very elderly, so they constitute a higher proportion of people experiencing these kinds of conditions. Accidents at work have been replaced by accidents on the roads. A much higher proportion of male drivers are involved in road accidents than female drivers: a road safety survey in 1988 found that just under one-half of all male drivers were involved in road accidents, as against just over one-quarter of female drivers. Young men would appear to be more vulnerable to being injured in this way, perhaps because the fast motor car is sold as a symbol of power and virility. Technological advances, therefore, have not only improved conditions of life and work; they have also created new sets of problems and new disabling dangers. Health and safety laws regulate most places of work but are still hedged with qualifications which reduce their effectiveness and are often abused. Furthermore, they do not always cover the places of work in which women predominate (Bisset and Huws, 1984).

Technological advances have also occurred in medical science. At the same time as changing conditions of work and living, they have changed the practice of medicine and have enabled the treatment of many illnesses and diseases. Over time and particularly during the course of the twentieth century, illness and disability have come to be redefined as a medical issue rather than a moral or secular one.

The medical model

The recent history of policy towards people with disabilities has been one of conceptualising disability as a tragic event happening to an individual who is medically diagnosed as 'suffering' from a particular condition or impairment, and who then becomes eligible for various forms of assistance. According to Scott (1970), the traditional view of such people has been to see them as 'helpless, dependants, incapable of mastering the elementary skills essential for engaging in productive social and economic activities'. The responsibility for giving support and care to people with disabilities originally lay with the family or, when they were poor, with the state, as described above. This century, however, the responsibility gradually shifted from the family and the state to a number of professionally trained people who claimed to have a special expertise in certain areas. In particular, medical doctors claimed an expertise and were given authority in relation to the body, its functioning and its impairments. Social workers, physiotherapists, speech therapists and others claimed other forms of expertise, and the industry of rehabilitation was born. But it was medical doctors who assumed prime responsibility, not only for sick people but also for people whose bodies were physically impaired.

Consequently, a medical model of disease developed which is characterised by Bury (1979) as following a course from aetiology to pathology to the manifestation of disease, with curative medicine intervening at the final point when the symptoms of the disease are manifested. The training of doctors and the medical culture that has developed around this has tended to emphasise biological know-ledge, giving paramount importance to the physiological features of illness and impairment. In a crude sense, the focus of attention (and indeed the division into medical specialities) has been less on a whole view of the person than a partial view of the eyes, ears, legs, joints, kidneys, etc. of the individual. In addition to this, a medical model of care has evolved which makes certain assumptions about the relationship between doctor and patient and the roles each is expected to play as they interact. This model of care has been further characterised as consisting of the following assumptions or rules (although, like most models, the characterisation is heuristic and somewhat rigid):

> The physician is the technically competent expert.
> ... the physician is the principal decision maker...
>> The patient is expected to assume the 'sick role' that requires him/her to co-operate with the medical practitioners caring for him/her.
>> The main purpose of medicine is the provision of acute/restorative care.
>> Illness is muted primarily through the use of clinical procedures such as surgery, drug therapy...
>> Illness can only be diagnosed, certified and treated by trained practitioners. (De Jong, 1981, p. 244).

This is a rather precise and perhaps more extended definition of the medical model than can be justified in practice. However, it would be fair to say that the medical model of care usually means that *physical* explanations are used to account for the effects of a person's impairment or for their disablement. In this respect, the physician is considered to be the prime possessor of knowledge about the impairment or illness, and this knowledge gives the physician some power over the impaired person. The 'patient' is there to recount or describe her or his symptoms and sensations and to assist the physician in making a diagnosis of the illness and prescribing treatment for it. In the process of diagnosing, people with disabilities are often given clinical labels. These labels have come to serve two functions outside medical care and treatment. They are used as administrative indications of need, legitimising and controlling someone's access to financial and other assistance. They also attach a stigma to the person so labelled by suggesting a physical imperfection or deviance from the norm.

The application of clinical labels to individuals can obscure the different dimensions that their impairment or disability takes and the different effects the same disease can have for different people. Multiple sclerosis is a good case in point, as the variability in the course it takes is one of its key characteristics. A certain indication of its prognosis is difficult to achieve (Robinson, 1988, p. 6). In this case, as in others, a medical diagnosis does not necessarily have any 'significant implications for each disabled person's career', as has been claimed (Royal College of Physicians, 1986, p. 5).

The medical model of care raises a number of issues regarding its appropriateness for assisting chronically ill or impaired people. The role of the doctor is generally based on acute illness, i.e. to identify or diagnose a person's illness and to sanction their release from normal social activities and obligations. After appropriate medical treatment, the sick person will be declared fit or cured and will be able to resume their normal everyday, but temporarily suspended, responsibilities. This presents a number of problems for people whose illnesses or impairments are permanent. First, they cannot be cured. Second, they do not necessarily exhibit symptoms which can be alleviated. Third, they do not usually wish or need to be relived of their normal activities, duties and responsibilities. Instead, they need whatever is required to be able to live continuously with their condition, and for that to be recognised and given legitimacy. In practice, the medical input for chronic illnesses or physical injuries is largely confined to the acute stages of the illness or injury, while the long-term management of it rests with the individuals and their families (Newman, 1984a).

A distinction does need to be made between a stable impairment and a moving impairment which is changing due to an underlying chronic condition. Newman (1984a) distinguishes chronic illnesses or impairments on the basis of the course they take, i.e. the rate and direction of progression. He makes a distinction between those with a 'downward trajectory' like multiple sclerosis or arthritis, and those with an 'upward trajectory' such as strokes or head injuries. The latter is usually occasioned by a traumatic event, rather like a spinal injury or polio. After the initial trauma, during which considerable medical intervention might be necessary, there are varying degrees of recovery, with the condition reaching a plateau which can remain relatively stable for the duration of that person's life. The former usually involves a slow and insidious deterioration in physical functioning which might or might not make more regular and more frequent demands on the medical profession.

This distinction has not always been recognised. On the one hand, all people with disabilities (whether these arise out of a stable impairment or a chronic illness) have tended to be categorised as being sick in the sense that they have a medical problem requiring the attention of a medical doctor. This is often implicit, as in the gatekeeping role which doctors are required to play in determining eligibility to certain benefits. Mobility Allowance illustrates this, as its rules insist that mobility be defined as a purely physiological process which medical doctors are called upon to judge. Hence people who are partially sighted or who have intellectual impairments have been excluded from receipt of the allowance. More recently there have been moves to recognise mobility as a more complex issue with a social dimension, such as the need that many intellectually impaired people have for assistance in going to places despite not having a medical or physiological problem of walking. Given the crucial nature of financial benefits in fostering independence and autonomy, the significance of the medical gatekeeper should not be underestimated (Stone, 1984).

As a reaction to this over-medicalised model of disability, disability is sometimes conceptualised in a way which seems to deny the 'downward trajectory' or any significant element of pain, sickness or morbidity (Brisenden, 1987). It is important, however, not .to return to the old post-war notion that someone with a disability is a young, otherwise healthy male with little need of doctors or health care, which often seems to be implicit in this view. There is exactly the opposite bias in the overall prevalence of physical impairment towards chronic, degenerative disease, particularly among older women. While three times as many men have injuries and amputations than women, people with chronic illnesses such as arthritis and multiple sclerosis tend to be women (Harris, 1971). Even the so-called 'young chronic sick' have a mean age of just over 50 years (Wood, 1978).

An adequate understanding of the experience of disabilities arising from illnesses and impairments with 'downward trajectories' will need to 'incorporate a careful consideration of the physical aspects of damage', as well as the social and economic aspects (Newman, 1984a). To deny the different objective and subjective realities of the different illnesses and impairments is to deny and devalue the authenticity of people's experiences (Abberley, 1987, p. 16). However, making these distinctions should not be mistaken for the application of a clinical label or for a purely disease-oriented approach which obscures the ubiquity of physical disability, i.e. the experience of stigma, exclusion, discrimination and dependency – all of which deprive people with disabilities from having control over their own lives.

The social model

People with physical disabilities are atypical in that they often appear different to others and may not be able to perform certain actions within a range that is considered normal for someone of their age. Some writers have suggested that they therefore represent a threat to the social order as well as a less valued group within it (Scambler, 1984). Their impairment or disability is a quality which both stigmatises them and entitles them to special treatment. Throughout history, people with disabilities have confronted an ambivalence in the attitudes of others towards them, of fear mingled with concern. At different times the pendulum of policy has swung more towards incorporating attitudes of fear, and at other times towards incorporating attitudes of concern, e.g. when the birth of children with disabilities was regarded as a good omen for the community (Scott, 1970). The possession of a disability was more commonly, and sometimes still is, regarded as evidence of divine punishment or retribution for sins committed either in a previous life or by one's forebearers. Although, officially, blame is no longer laid at the door of individuals in this way, the notion of moral culpability is still present in social attitudes and beliefs, however sub-conscious and irrational this may be. In the consumer-oriented societies of the West, where a high value is placed on youth and physical beauty and where goods are often sold by creating an association between them and a particular style of alleged physical beauty, the moral culpability also has to do with *not* fulfilling the requirements to be 'beautiful'. Chapter 4 argues that this has a particular impact on women with disabilities.

Nowadays, formal policy has moved on from overtly attributing blame and guilt to asserting a more paternalistic approach in which the care and support of people with physical disabilities has been placed in the hands of professionally trained people. The model is based on a view of the amenable and conscientious professional working on behalf of the client in this case the person who has a disability towards agreed goals (Barton, 1986). Their task is generally seen to be one of helping people overcome problems which are perceived to arise out of their disabilities. People with disabilities are no longer to blame, but they now have a problem. Their mark or stigma of being impaired is an important part of their being ascribed the role of deviant.

In her study of the provision of services for people with disabilities in a Scottish city, Blaxter (1976) found that the most expensive goods, such as adapted motor cars and complex equipment, were in the control of the higher-status professions in medicine who would act as gatekeepers in prescribing these for people on the basis of their clinical judgement. She suggests that this had more to do with professional politics than a rational assessment of need. It was also found to be a method of rationing demand and minimising complaints about their allocation. Interestingly, she found that people with disabilities preferred to enter the system of provision through health rather than welfare agencies, which reflects possibly a realistic assessment on their part of the greater power of medical gatekeepers.

According to Becker (1963, p. 8) deviance is not necessarily due to the actions of a person but is a label which has been applied to certain individuals or groups. It is, therefore, a 'consequence of the application by others, of rules and sanctions to an offender. The deviant is one to whom that label has successfully been applied.' As deviants, they are subject to exclusion from normal social and public life. This is manifested in inaccessible buildings, by being regarded as fire hazards in public places, and by overt and covert discrimination. Under current British judicial practice, for example. someone with a disability may be barred from jury service on account of that disability, regardless of whether it has an effect on their capacity for reasoning.

Someone considered to be deviant may also be subject to various forms of social control such as involuntary institutionalisation or sterilisation, as has happened to some women with intellectual disabilities. As is shown in Chapter 4, some attempts to cure or 'make normal' certain disabilities rather than accommodating them are also forms of social control. Scott (1970, p. 113) suggests that the underlying reason for the need to exert control over people considered to be deviant, is that the deviant makes the rest of society uneasy, their very existence questioning the existing order and threatening any sense of mastery over nature.

The extent of stigmatisation and deviance experienced by someone will vary according to the type and extent of their disability. Furnham and Pendred (1983), in a study of attitudes towards people with disabilities, suggest that people have more positive attitudes towards physical disability than mental disability. Sutherland (1981, p. 14) demonstrates how the visibility of a disability or impairment contributes towards defining someone's status as a disabled person. In his study of stigma, Goffman (1968, p. 65) suggests that the visibility of a particular stigma will be crucial in determining its effect on an individual. He distinguishes four issues which influence its visibility and which have particular relevance to physical disability. They are the extent to which it is evident, the extent to which it is known about, its obtrusiveness, and its perceived focus. Physical impairments such as epilepsy, diabetes or stammering are not always either evident or known about, and until they become so, may not be stigmatising.

The extent of stigmatisation will also vary according to particular circumstances and the obtrusiveness of certain disabilities. In some situations, one particular disability may draw more attention and be more discomforting to others than another. Goffman (1968, p. 66) illustrates this by reference to a business meeting, in which a person in a wheelchair is very little different to other participants compared to a person with a marked speech impediment. However, in attempting to catch a bus, the occupant of the wheelchair will be significantly more noticeable and more handicapped than the person with the speech impediment, who is more likely to 'pass' as a typical passenger. The importance of the social context in transforming an impairment into a disabling or handicapping condition also extends to the perceptions that people have about how certain groups should look or behave. Norms of femininity or masculinity are also likely to influence whether, and the extent to which, an individual is stigmatised by their impairment.

People whose disability is perceived by others to disqualify them from certain spheres of activity will also experience a greater stigma, according to Goffman, and therefore their disability will have a greater effect on their lives. However, this is likely to take different forms. For example, someone with facial scarring may be disqualified from most social situations because they are perceived as threatening. Someone who is blind, however, may not be considered socially threatening but may experience great difficulty in getting employment.

A study of one hundred and fifty largely young, white corporation managers in the United States gives some evidence for the differential impact of obviously visible disabilities. The study tested the perceived social distance of the managers from people with a variety of physical disabilities and with other stigmatising conditions such as drug abuse and homosexuality. People with disabilities were considered more acceptable than these other groups, but the visibility of their disability affected the extent of that acceptability. The managers expressed a greater distance between themselves and people with visible, functional incapacities and were more likely to reject people with visible disfigurements, for instance, than with less obvious degenerative conditions (Albrecht *et al.*, 1982). Although they may have expressed greater rejection of drug abusers or homosexuals, these groups are more able to 'pass' as typical than many disabled people.

Ambiguity in social interaction was the most frequent reason given for this rejection. This ambiguity included feelings of fear and unfamiliarity with the disability as well as expressions of ignorance about the disabled person's condition. The able-bodied managers did not know how to interact and when to offer help, their rejection appearing to be a reflection of their own inadequacy in certain situations.

Feelings of fear, ignorance and unfamiliarity with physical disability stem from a lack of integration between disabled and non-disabled people. However, the stigmatisation of people with disabilities that results from this in turn creates yet more barriers to their acceptance and integration in society. The exclusion and segregation of people with disabilities begins in school and continues into employment. It is further exacerbated by an inaccessible environment which is hostile to people who have difficulties in mobility.

4

Invisible women

Very little attention has been devoted to the situation of women who are disabled, and what does exist has usually been written by the women themselves. There has been little scientific work or systematic study of the circumstances and needs of women who are born or become disabled either in the USA (Mudrick, 1983a) or in the UK (Campling, 1981a). This is possibly due to a view that it is more acceptable for a women to become disabled because passivity, docility and dependency are more compatible with the female sex role. Similarly, the loss of paid employment may be perceived to be less traumatic for women because they are seen to rely on it less and to have an alternative role in the home as homemaker (Safilios-Rothschild, 1977; Brown and Rawlinson, 1977; Kutner and Gray, 1981). The consequences of this are that in the literature on disability, women are all but invisible. In recent years, this has slowly begun to change, but it is still commonplace for large-scale studies to ignore the effect of gender. The work that has been done on women and disability has tended to consist of personal accounts or small-scale qualitative studies.

Women with disabilities are rendered invisible in a host of different ways. First, they actually appear less and are, literally, seen less often in public. Second, even when they are not physically out of sight, they are psychologically out of sight. Third, as a minority group, they are often ignored and devalued by the majority. This chapter will consider each of these in turn, focusing on two particular services which have contributed to the process of rendering women with disabilities invisible. Rehabilitation services

42

have traditionally been geared towards the needs of men and have, therefore, impeded the integration of women into mainstream society. Medical services, by treating *conditions* rather than *people*, have cast women into passive roles in which things are done *to* them rather than *with* them. the media and advertising have largely ignored people with disabilities as valid and valuable constituencies.

Out of sight, out of mind

There are millions of people in Britain who are disabled, who are never seen. The reason they are never seen is that they have no means of *being* seen. They live in inadequate housing, they have no facilities for transport to get to the places they want to go to. They cannot go to a cinema. I haven't been in a cinema for years. There are only about two theatres in London that I can go to – the National and the Barbican. This does not just cut across my life, it cuts across family life as well, as opportunities for doing things together are drastically curtailed. You learn to live with it and tell yourself that it doesn't matter – but it does (Davoud, 1985, p. 146).

The invisibility of many women starts with their schooling. Because of long periods of hospitalisation, some children with disabilities are tutored at home. The presenting crisis of their illness or the immediate needs of their impairment may lead to a neglect of their educational needs. Other children are usually sent to special schools where their education takes place in a segregated setting, out of the sight of other children. The effect of most segregation is to keep the separated group hidden from the view of other people. Most importantly, segregation retards understanding. The vast majority of women who were interviewed for this book felt that non-disabled people should be educated alongside people with disabilities right from the start. One young woman, Swasti, having had all her schooling at a special school, found the transition to an ordinary college very difficult because of the lack of understanding of her fellow students:

I don't think it's fair to the able-bodied for us to go to special schools, because they don't know how to go about it, they don't know how to talk to you. They haven't had any contact either, same as you. It makes you unapproachable. They don't know how to. You're very visible but you're unapproachable.

Women are not only unseen as children. Because they are restricted in getting employment, they are often not seen as adults either. Since only 9 per cent of women with disabilities are employed (Buckle, 1971) this often means being at home all day, every day. The 8 per cent of elderly women who live segregated in institutions also remain out of the public eye for most of their lives. Housing is an enormous problem for many people with disabilities, who can wait years to be allocated appropriate housing. Buckle found that 15 per cent of local authority tenants and 34 per cent of private tenants had been waiting for over five years to be housed or rehoused. Over half of private tenants had been waiting for more than ten years. Yet inappropriate housing can make people unnecessarily housebound or restrict them from going out. It can also make day-to-day tasks more time-consuming than necessary, again making it more difficult to go out. In one study (Locker, 1983) several women complained of such a hazard. Their flats were awkwardly and inappropriately designed: kitchens, for instance, were conventionally designed with no modifications for someone with a disability.

Housing schemes designed specifically with the needs of people with disabilities in mind have attempted to overcome some of the difficulties of modifying unsuitable houses. While they have often overcome both the need for, and the worst effects of, institutionalised living, they do not truly integrate people into the community. They serve to increase someone's independence but not necessarily their visibility.

An issue which arose a number of times during the interviews for this book was whether women with disabilities should raise the subject of their disability with other people. Antoinette found it difficult to cope with the reticence of some people (which she saw as being part of traditional, white, British culture) to talk about her very obvious impairment:

> I think most black people don't mind asking us what's wrong. And how does it affect you if you can't walk? I think it is [easier] if you get that over and done with at the beginning. Rather than them thinking about it. Especially if they know they can ask you anything, they don't have to feel their way round it. In America, too, they are very open. Britain is a very conservative nation.

In contrast, Margaret found that her impairment, which isn't immediately obvious until she has to do something with her arms, presented her with another type of problem:

I've had the option open to me of being able to disguise my disability in the initial contacts. If you're wheelchair-bound, you can't. I can meet people and talk – people have often met me on quite a number of occasions before they realise I have a disability. That's a problem for me. Particularly at that stage of my life [going to university]. It didn't seem natural to me to say 'Hi, I'm Margaret, I'm disabled, do you want to know all about it?' On the other hand, particularly with boys, I knew I hung back because I didn't want people to feel they had been conned. I found that very difficult – wanting people to meet me and know what they needed to know without making a big thing of it.

What both women seem to be dealing with is the inability of the non-disabled world to accept the physical differences of this particular minority, and the uncertainty which this generates for them. Their experiences reflect the ambiguity and potential social disruption which Goffman (1968) suggests is present when stigmatised and non-stigmatised people interact. It reflects an anxiety on both sides about whether or not to acknowledge the disability and how to deal with the new social roles which this will entail for both parties. Some women whose disability was literally invisible, spoke of the relief they felt at making their disability known and at no longer having to carry the burden of their 'secret' around with them. Nadia, for instance, spoke of her sense of liberation at 'coming out' as disabled, of telling people that she had multiple sclerosis and of both educating them about it and, at the same time, making herself more visible.

Others felt that it was the responsibility of the woman who is disabled to make herself visible. For instance, in looking for employment, Anita said she thought women who are disabled should try to go along to employment agencies and let them see that they're around and looking for work. Debra said that in certain situations she tries to mix and make herself as visible as possible:

You must go and make yourself known to people. I see so many people sitting out there in chairs who won't mix. We have to try and develop a few tricks to get people talking to you more easily, if you're doing the work I'm doing. So, that's one of my tricks, to go and introduce myself at lunchtime. You can feel their reaction to you. And being the first in. That throws people. But it sets them off talking to you. A lot of disabled people just sit and wait for people to come to them.

While Debra was annoyed at the inaccessibility of many places and the enforced social isolation which she often had to confront, another woman, Sheila, had not regarded her invisibility just as a problem. She saw it as having certain positive elements:

> The positive thing, I suppose, is you get to observe people. I suppose you're an outsider, really. I think I can observe people. I can be more observant of situations.

Rehabilitation

The rehabilitation services have played a particular role in neglecting to recognise the needs of women. The reason for this can be found in the origins of these services. Policies for vocational rehabilitation have usually been more forthcoming after a period of war, when injury casualty rates have been high. For instance, the Lord Roberts' Workshops were established to help meet the occupational needs of men returning injured from the Boer War, and the present government skillcentres were established in 1919 to retrain injured men from the 1914–18 war. The major impetus for rehabilitation policy in both the USA and Britain occurred after the Second World War, as evidenced in the establishment of the veterans' administration service in the USA and the British resettlement services. This has not been something particular to Western industrialised countries. Zimbabwean social policy was notable for its concentration on disability after its protracted war of independence. Likewise, most of the co-operatives for workers with disabilities in Poland were established by and for those injured during the Second World War.

It is not difficult to see why this should have been so. When people's disabilities are seen to have been caused while in service to their country, there is usually political and moral appeal in providing for their needs. In addition to this, during the Second World War in Britain, the shortage of labour in production industries due to mobilisation gave added impetus to a rehabilitation service which could get disabled men back to work if they could no longer fight.

Even before this, though, precedence had been given to the war disabled in social security and some social services. This has led to a particular view of disability which is associated with the predominantly male pursuit of war and the resulting war veterans. In addition to focusing on war disablement, rehabilitation and resettlement has tended to concentrate on employment. In a society which does not perceive women to be the 'natural' breadwinners, such a focus is more likely to disadvantage them, as indeed is the provision of social security benefits linked to employment records. Services and benefits which are related to participation in the military or industrial sphere are likely to have less relevance for women. These developments have encouraged a whole framework of provision which is blinkered to the needs of women with disabilities and which gives less consideration to planning for their long-term futures (as well as more immediate adjustments) than would have been given to men with disabilities. Blaxter (1976, p. 158) found evidence of this in her study. Official agencies assumed that women had alternatives to paid employment or that they would solve their problems in an informal way. Women were encouraged to remain idle whether they wanted to or not, and in any event had less contact with the Disablement Resettlement Officer, whether registered or not.

Stereotyping according to sex and/or disability is an extremely effective means of proscribing the labour market or sections of the labour market. When racial stereotypes are added to the equation, the combination can be devastating. Vash (1982) documents how useful this process has been during times of labour surplus such as after the Second World War. She points to the irony of vocational rehabilitation schemes burgeoning alongside attempts to exclude women with disabilities from the labour force: 'while one hand pulled and kept disabled workers out of the competitive labour market, the other hand built vocational rehabilitation as a sizeable peacetime industry.' However, rehabilitation itself grew out of a concern for the war disabled, most of whom have always been male. This association with the predominantly male pursuit of war and resulting male war veterans has led to a service in which the involvement of women is inhibited.

Britain's rehabilitation and resettlement service had its foundations in the Tomlinson Committee, established during the Second World War, and the 1944 Disabled Persons (Employment) Act, although the legislative basis for industrial rehabilitation was replaced in 1973 by the Employment and Training Act. This laid a duty on a branch of the Department of Employment, the Manpower Services Commission, to make appropriate provision for 'assisting persons to select, train for, obtain and retain employment suitable for their ages and capacities' (Manpower Services Commission, 1981, p. 9). The original model was undoubtedly therapeutic and individualistic, based on the onset of disability being sudden, e.g. through war or industrial injury, rather than gradual, as are degenerative diseases such as multiple sclerosis or arthritis – two diseases most prevalent among women.

The first industrial rehabilitation centre was established in 1943, although government training centres had already been in existence since 1919 for men disabled in the First World War. Today there are twenty-seven employment rehabilitation centres (ERCs) and four residential training colleges for people with disabilities. Like special schools, they represent a form of segregated provision, although the length of time of a training course is relatively short. The courses generally concentrate on rehabilitation for manual or lower-level skilled jobs. Together with other legislative policy which designates the posts of car park attendant and lift operator as solely for people who are disabled, this perpetuates a low-status occupational pattern for people with disabilities. It also encourages low expectations of people who are disabled and contributes towards the downward mobility that is often attendant upon becoming disabled.

At any one time, there are about 2,000 people attending employment rehabilitation centres in Britain. About 14,000 – 15,000 people complete courses at such centres each year (Manpower Services Commission, 1984). Despite the number of women in the labour market increasing sharply since the Second World War, a study undertaken in 1980 found that this increase was not reflected in a commensurate increase in the proportion or numbers of women attending courses at employment rehabilitation centres (Somerville, 1980). Over the decade 1970 – 1980, women formed only 12 per cent of the total number of rehabilitants, although women and men with disabilities of working age are roughly equal in number. This contrasts sharply with the USA, where the proportion of women and men who are referred for, and receive, vocational training is roughly equal. There, the number of white women referred tends to be slightly less than white men, and the number of black women slightly more than black men. However, an analysis of over 4,500 disabled adults found that the type of rehabilitation men and women received was different, as was the result. Women received fewer work related services and returned less often to paid employment, suggesting that a stereotype regarding the role of women and employment may have been influencing the rehabilitation process (Mudrick, 1987).

In Britain the minority status of women in rehabilitation centres partly reflects the low incidence of women in the paid labour force, as well as the fact that they tend to use the public employment services less than men. Somerville suggests that two other factors play a part in discouraging women from using rehabilitation facilities. One is that the work done in them is perceived to be men's work by both public referral agencies (Disablement Resettlement Officers) and the women themselves. Another is that they are oriented towards resettlement into full-time employment (Somerville, 1980). Both factors have been thought to deter women from participating in other training and apprenticeship schemes which have not provided non-traditional skills training, part-time training, childcare facilities, and practices which are more sympathetic to the ways in which women live and work (Wickham, 1982).

Women who do attend the rehabilitation centres tend to be young (under 25), single, unqualified, and living with their parents. This is in sharp contrast to male clients, who tend to be older and married with family responsibilities (Somerville, 1980). This suggests that rehabilitation may not be addressing or meeting the needs of older women who wish to return to employment after an absence from it, because of either child-rearing or their disability. It also suggests that in the referral process to a rehabilitation centre, a stereotyped view prevails that married men with disabilities need rehabilitation and retraining courses while married women with disabilities do not. The difference in age and marital status of women undertaking such rehabilitation from the overall population of women with disabilities of working age seems to be another example of general attitudes towards, and expectations of, women.

When in the rehabilitation centre, women tend to undertake a narrower variety of work than men, largely light or menial work. Three-quarters of the women in Somerville's study attended sections doing packaging or assembly work, compared to one-third of the men. Only 10 per cent of women were allocated to woodwork or machine-operating sections of the workshop, and none to the bench engineering section which over one-third of the men attended. This reflects general patterns of occupational segregation in the labour market and is part of a wider pattern of work whereby women not only do different jobs to men but do more menial and lower-paid jobs (Hakim, 1978, 1981).

Success for many people in rehabilitation (especially for women and black people) is closely associated with rehabilitation personnel and their values, attitudes and beliefs. In Somerville's study, women clients were better liked by their instructors than were men clients. Instructors also reported feeling more protective towards them. However, these preferences and paternal feelings seem not to have had an effect on the women's performance. Female clients were not rated as highly as male clients in all aspects of workshop performance, i.e. motivation, work standards, work speed, efforts, control of emotions and responses to instructions (although in some respects younger males were similarly poorly rated, making it difficult to separate the influence of age and gender). In later assessments the social and emotional performance ratings of women improved.

It may be that different judgements are being made in respect of the rehabilitation goals envisaged for men and women. This emerges in the final reports in which men and women are judged suitable for different jobs. No woman was thought capable of skilled work, whereas over half the men were. Men were more likely to receive recommendations for skilled or semi-skilled manual work or at least for further training in such work. It is difficult to know whether these low expectations had an effect on the women's careers. Six months after completing rehabilitation courses, however, 38 per cent of women and 48 per cent of men were either in employment or on training courses. The remainder were sick or unemployed (Somerville, 1980).

These rehabilitation services were evaluated internally in 1981 and reforms proposed in 1984. The position of women appears not to have been considered, nor were any recommendations made about improving their participation in relevant rehabilitation programmes. This is surprising considering the important observations of Somerville's study and other work which is stressing the lack of awareness and sensitivity to women's aspirations and the special rehabilitation and employment needs of women and mothers with disabilities (Stace, 1986; Perry, 1984; Atkins, 1982; Thurer, 1982).

Similar evidence is emerging in the USA regarding the relative position of men and women in rehabilitation. Mary Croxon John reports a study undertaken in 1987 of the rehabilitation services in six states. Important differences were found in the characteristics, service patterns and outcomes of rehabilitation for women and men. After vocational rehabilitation, women earned less, had a greater possibility of falling below the poverty level, achieved less financial independence, and were more reliant on public assistance. This occurred even when their financial resources had been similar to men at the start of the programme, and when they had entered it with higher levels of education than men. In addition to this, referral systems were found to favour young men, presumably reflecting views about priority groups for employment. None of the vocational rehabilitation programmes had formulated systematic approaches that would address the vocational experience and characteristics of women (John, 1988).

In her own study of rehabilitation centres in Europe, Croxon John (1988, p. 101) found that women were seen as a poor rehabilitation risk, which probably accounted for the fewer numbers of women that were found in vocational training programmes; those that were tended to be single. Little account had been taken of women's family commitments. Women were going into traditionally female courses, and the European Centre for Vocational Training had undertaken no initiatives on the particular training needs of women.

Rehabilitation and getting paid work are only part of the story. Vash (1982) makes a useful distinction between employment and a career, the latter being the vocational path which 'will best facilitate self-actualisation as personally defined'. Women with disabilities have the same right as anyone else not only to paid work if they want it, but also to a livelihood which is rewarding and enriching at all levels. This means having a real choice of job in an area not traditional to either women or people with disabilities, as well as the possibility of promotion and change. For women with disabilities, this means having additional internal resources to cope with discrimination and prejudice if they encounter it, and external resources such as aids, adaptations and support systems. Perry's study found that the barriers to making a real choice of career or change in career were not only to be found in the world at large but in the perception women with disabilities had internalised about themselves (Perry, 1984, p. 14). The biggest challenge may be in relation to women with intellectual disabilities who face some of the greatest prejudices of all.

Although the effectiveness of rehabilitation courses in assisting people to obtain jobs is not great (in 1982, 47 per cent of rehabilitants at employment rehabilitation centres were still unemployed one year after the course), no systematic study seems to have been undertaken which compares their career paths with those who have not undertaken such courses. In the United States, however, one study has made a comparison in relation to the percentage employed and their average earnings. While there were wide variations across the different states, as a whole rehabilitants had better records of employment and earnings. The relative impact of rehabilitation was generally more positive for women (Greenblum, 1977). This suggests that rehabilitation is potentially of great importance to women, possibly because of their earlier neglect in education and training.

Medical care

Women often have very different ways of defining the nature, context and management of their disabilities than their doctors. They have to negotiate an environment full of barriers, which consumes time, energy and money, often leading to what Locker (1983, p. 90) calls a 'state of enforced passivity'. The dominance of medicine has led to the medical condition of people with disabilities being defined as *the* problem at hand, rather than the social and economic barriers which confront them. Consequently, whether they need it or not, many people with disabilities come into frequent and often prolonged contact with the health care services and professionals. Although this contact is often necessary and helpful, it is equally often traumatic, and the service provided is often inappropriate.

The women in this study regularly reported bad experiences of health professionals, in particular doctors, describing them as punitive, patronising, dismissive and unhelpful, with one woman saying she felt she 'survived in spite of them'. Every now and then a woman might have come across a general practitioner or a consultant who was helpful and acted in partnership with them. The gratitude, enthusiasm and warmth with which these women described such contacts suggest that they are rare encounters. The problems seem to be (a) the inability of doctors to deal with conditions that are incurable; (b) the desire of doctors for a high degree of compliance; (c) doctors not acknowledging their ignorance at certain times, nor the possibility that women, who have been disabled for some time, may know a great deal about that condition; (d) the lack of practical information possessed by doctors to pass on to their disabled patients; and (e) doctors generally being male and having stereotyped views of women.

The health culture into which women with disabilities must step, by and large sees doctors as curers, and nurses, paramedicals and auxiliaries as carers. One women described the effect of this on health staff as follows:

> I think that medics, consultants, physiotherapists, the general hospital staff find it very difficult to deal with a permanent disability, something that they can't actually cure. I think it makes them feel invalid. And because of that, that they can't do anything, it then comes back on to the patients. It's that sort of relationship that develops. Whereas the more basic grade staff are not really involved at that level of care, their level of care is very much more practical, and you can establish a better relationship. I just feel that the medics were basically trying to cure you.

The confusion between illness and disability creates a number of problems for people learning to live with a physical disability that has a stable trajectory. Much sickness or ill-health is an undesirable state of affairs, and people generally expect and look forward to the time when health will be regained. By contrast, physically disabling conditions are permanent and do not always exhibit any serious or debilitating medical symptoms. People generally adapt and live with their disability, and do not strive against it in a fruitless attempt to be able-bodied. What is appropriate behaviour by and towards the temporarily sick person, may be entirely dysfunctional for the person with a disability, even when it is accompanied by a permanent state of ill health. For those people whose disability is a chronic illness such as arthritis or multiple sclerosis, the notion of being cured or made well (while a possibility) may be less relevant on a daily level, where adaptation and accommodation to the disability is necessary.

Some women felt that the desire to cure them was a denial of their validity as they actually were. It was also seen to reflect a desire to turn disabled women into able-bodied women, and that, in some instances, this had led to them having to undergo unnecessary surgical procedures. One woman with cerebral palsy felt that an operation to her legs using normal orthopaedic treatment that would have been used on someone who had accidentally broken both legs, was inappropriate for her body which had developed its particular shape through spasms. She was also angry at having been given physiotherapy and exercises when she felt that occupational therapy and a proper education would have been more relevant to helping her make her way in the world. She believed the doctors were trying to turn her into something she wasn't instead of teaching her to use what capabilities she had to her best advantage. Moreover, she felt that various operations to her hip had left her more disabled than before, without doing anything to assist her to live a full life as someone with cerebral palsy. Prior to the operation she described being able to use a walking frame to get herself into bed and to transfer on and off the toilet. After the operation, she could do neither. Another woman, Anita, on the other hand, had been undergoing surgery for her arthritis for most of her life, and this now enabled her to sit in a wheelchair and even to walk periodically rather than being bedridden.

Whether or not surgery is necessary depends on the nature of the condition being treated and the skill of the surgeon. It is certainly possible that some surgery is undertaken for the wrong reasons, without any consultation with the women being operated on. To some extent, the desire to cure may be part of a broader and more complex pressure which many minorities experience to assimilate into the majority. In a study of blindness, Deshen and Deshen (1989, p. 94) found that the stigma attaching to people with disabilities extended to their appliances. A number of people in their study reported being pressurised by friends and families to try to walk without their white canes.

Doctors and compliance

Some doctors expect a certain type of behaviour from their patients, becoming extremely patronising in their attitudes towards women who do not behave in that way. One woman said she had always felt that she must present a 'Little Miss Sunshine' image because the consequences were so bad when she did not:

I had a terrible GP here. The two of us were like knives at each other. He threatened to smack my bottom. I was over thirty. I said, I should like to see you try. I thought, I'll beat this man up. Poor –[her partner]– burst into tears.

A couple of women said they felt that the very behaviour which would stand them in good stead, in trying to survive and cope, was discouraged by doctors and nurses. 'Bad' behaviour in their terms was being independent, highly motivated to help oneself, active and even aggressive. Being a 'good' patient was being passive and obedient. Jule said she felt constrained to be pleasant, and that 'the expectations were that you should smile'. She found that her lack of co-operation was frowned on: 'I was known as being rather unco-operative, which probably meant I was trying hard to survive.'

Saviola (1981) makes a similar point regarding women who are leaving or wish to leave a hospital or institutional setting. Behaviour traits such as aggression or assertiveness that would be taboo in the institution, are considered to be the very traits needed for independent living. The desire for compliance is also reflected in the status that is associated with being a professional, especially a doctor. Doctors are meant to be all-knowing and therefore find it difficult to acknowledge ignorance on some matters. This status is not conducive to working jointly with patients and consulting with them at all stages of the treatment or management process. Many women with disabilities feel that they have a good understanding of their needs since their disability is something that never leaves them and is part of their lives, but this is not always recognised by doctors who may only come into their lives briefly. This was clearly illustrated by Enid's doctor:

When I had one abcess and went to the hospital the doctor said, 'You'll have to have a general anaesthetic.' I said, 'I won't, I'm totally paralysed, I won't feel a thing.' So, there was this big argument. I thought, why take the risk of a general anaesthetic when it's not needed? Eventually, I persuaded him – even so, he gave me a pain-killing injection in my bottom, totally useless, and afterwards he was talking to the other doctors and said, 'Well, you see, I did not have to give a general anaesthetic because this woman is paraplegic.' But he hadn't known, I'd had to tell him. A general anaesthetic wasn't necessary, and also, having asthma, I'm always a bit nervous of them. They said, 'But it's going to be very painful.' I said, 'Look, if I could feel I would be in agony now, wouldn't I, with the abcess?'

Likewise, Swasti realised that she would have to take matters into her own hands and try new ways of managing her polio, new ways which at the same time were less disabling. Without consciously wanting to do so, it is possible that some doctors perpetuate dependency by being unable to overcome their own limitations and recognise that their patients have a great deal of experience to offer to the healing or management process.

> I used to wear two callipers, and I always thought I didn't need two. I had to suggest that maybe I should try one. As opposed to them picking it up that the leg was strong enough. And it worked. After that I was on one calliper. I think you have to be aware of what you've got and what you can do. If you feel something, you have to try it. It might not be right, but it's worth it to try.

Few women thought they had been properly consulted by their doctors, and many thought that their doctors felt that, as professional people, they knew what was best for them. They felt that disabled people could have very little say in the way they were treated. Some women felt this would not change unless there was some way in which people with disabilities were incorporated into the decision-making process themselves. In Antoinette's case, her treatment was not only prescribed with no consultation, but also with no information about the side-effects she could expect, which were to make her sleepy and passive.

> I used to have severe pains in my hips, and my GP gave me a series of painkillers which didn't do anything for me. And then, some tablets he gave me, I thought they were strong painkillers, and my aunt, who is a nurse, said they were also a sleeping tablet. I was constantly taking these things. She said I should try and get off them or I would get hooked. I didn't believe her until I tried to come off them and I couldn't. I had withdrawal symptoms. Then he gave me another tablet which had codeine in it. I am allergic to aspirin.

If this type of poor quality care continues, more and more women are likely to be driven away from the health service. Antoinette did in fact change to a homeopathic doctor who she felt consulted with her more than orthodox doctors did.

> I went to see the homeopathic doctor who is also an osteopath, and have been going there ever since. It has helped. He doesn't make any decisions behind my back. If he finds something, he'll talk to me about it. He gives me the facts as they are. And then it's up to me to decide. Which other doctors or the GP never did.

Need for information

A number of women expressed the need for someone to talk to or for counselling at various times in their life. They also expressed the need for greater information about their disabilities, the services available to them, and how they could avail themselves of various facilities. One such time when help is needed is at the onset of the disabling condition. One woman who had gradually been losing her hearing since she was eighteen, had had no follow-up service since the date when she was informed of her diagnosis some twenty years ago. She had found the information traumatic and needed to talk to someone about the drastic change this was to make to her life. Many other women felt the need for some form of counselling, and one woman suggested that an outreach service would have helped to locate those women who needed such assistance.

> I'd have liked a bit of psychological back-up, when things were so bad as they were then. With Mummy with her stroke. She lived here as well at one time. And [her husband] in depression. And me flat on my back, all at the same time. I could have done with a bit of help from a social worker in understanding it from everybody's point of view. Everyone needed their needs attended to. I see it clearly now, but I didn't as easily then. We all needed help.

A study of the attitudes of general practitioners towards epilepsy found that although almost all the doctors in the study felt they were in a position to counsel patients, general practitioner counselling was generally poor, and alternative forms of professional counselling non-existent. Doctors were found to concentrate entirely on technical aspects of seizure control, ignoring and even resisting psycho-social issues (Davies and Scambler, 1988).

The lack of having someone to talk to can lead to great loneliness. In some situations it may be most appropriate to talk to other women in similar circumstances. Nadia found great comfort in linking up with other women who had also recently been diagnosed as having multiple sclerosis.

> I realised how dreadfully alone I was. We all of us felt the same. We 'phoned each other. Anything to just have somebody to talk to that would understand.

A particular time when counselling would be helpful is at adolescence. One young nineteen-year-old spoke of the myriad issues confronting her at this particular time in her life. Although ambivalent about social workers, she expressed a strong desire to have one to speak to, and a preference for a social worker rather than a consultant. Given her anxiety about talking to professional people and the general concerns of adolescents anyway, this may be another situation where someone could benefit from talking to a group of young women in similar circumstances, not necessarily all with a physical disability but perhaps all of similar age.

> I keep meaning to go to these advice things, but it's very hard to do that. I mean it's bad enough sitting here telling you, you know, let alone these high-powered specialist people. I do want a social worker to be honest because I do feel that you get further with a social worker. You do get certain priorities.

An issue which repeatedly came up in the interviews was how frightening most women's hospital experience had been for them, especially as children. Many studies have documented the stress and anxiety associated with hospitalisation, as well as the loss of privacy and independence (Newman, 1984b). For Debra, the combination of this with a harsh and almost punitive regime led to a complete breakdown in her sense of trust of others at a time when most children are developing just such a sense of trust and security (Marinelli and Dell Orto, 1977):

> I'd never been in hospital before. I don't remember much of the first month. I was in an iron lung. I remember being very frightened. And mother was allowed to stay with me for a lot of the time. I had some nasty incidents with one or two of the ward sisters who didn't understand what was happening to me. They should have had me in an iron lung, I understand, hours before they did. And they had to keep me awake. One of these sisters came on duty and said I should be asleep. So she shut all the lights out, turned my mother out, and left me in the dark. I was totally paralysed, and I hadn't enough breath to call. So, from then on for that month in the lung I lost all trust in the people around me. I couldn't help myself.

Miller and Gwynne (1972, p. 120) suggest that if children are separated from their parents by long spells of hospitalisation, they will feel they are being punished for bad behaviour or even for having a disability. They found evidence for this both at the level of fantasy and as a reality among people who had spent long spells in hospitals or homes from birth or in their early childhood. Margaret related a similar feeling of rejection when she was left in an isolation hospital as a child when she contracted polio:

I can remember to this day being left in a glass cubicle, just me in the bed, and I can see my mother walking away. I think that's why I feel so strongly about what happens to children in hospitals these days.

Jule also spoke of the little contact she had been allowed with her family, and of the routinised, structured and institutionalised regime of the hospital in which she had been:

It was not a happy time to remember. I can understand how long periods of separation from the family influences the way you feel about your own security. The old assumption that children cope very well in times of stress, I think is misguided. I feel children cope with what they are confronted with, but underneath they still need a lot of emotional support. I think in hospitals that is absent.

A devalued image

Attitudes towards people with disabilities have been mixed. On the one hand, they are seen as helpless dependants who are incapable of engaging in ordinary social life, let alone productive economic life, which leads to their isolation and segregation from the community. On the other hand, they are viewed with a mixture of hostility and fear which is relatively easy to repress because of their invisibility. Attitudes also differ with regard to men and women with disabilities, which reflect the different social and economic roles men and women perform in society. This can best be illustrated by the popular images portrayed of people with disabilities in literature and the media.

Men with disabilities are often portrayed as villains such as Richard III, Captain Hook, Dr Strangelove and Dr No, or monsters such as The Hunchback of Notre Dame and The Phantom of the Opera (Longmore, 1985). By contrast, women with disabilities are hardly depicted at all. If they are, it is not as admired heroine but as victim, such as the blind women attacked in the thriller *Wait until Dark*. One departure from this stereotype was a film depicting its heroine, Rosa Luxemburg, with a severe limp, although this was not dealt with as an issue by the film. The dominant images, however, mirror the roles that are expected of men and women. These are that women must be passive and invisible and expressive, while men must be active and aggressive and instrumental (Weitzman, 1979).

Hostility towards men with disabilities, therefore, is expressed by portraying them as doing evil, whereas towards women it is portrayed as having evil done to them.

It has been argued that the basis for this malign element of the stereotype lies in beliefs about the moral culpability of the person who is disabled. The disability is seen as '*prima facie* evidence of God's punishment for sinning' (Scott, 1970). One woman born with quadrilateral limb deficiencies writes of an exorcism being performed when she was brought home from hospital (Frank, 1984). According to Quicke (1985, p. 2), there are many ideas from past ages latent in the apparently progressive and realist societies of the West which still have considerable force. One of these is the notion 'legitimated by various religious teachings, that disability indicates possession by the devil or by an evil force, or is the outcome of evil doing'. A related belief was one reported by Swasti, who described how her mother believed that her daughter's polio was a punishment visited on her for wrongdoing in a previous life. Ironically, the more benign (but also negative) view of someone with a disability being passive and dependent is both an advance on such thinking and an attempt to defuse fears about disability by undermining the object of that fear.

A recent development in the USA relating to the image of people with disabilities has been the portrayal of people with disabilities in television commercials. One commercial for denim jeans showed a man in a wheelchair so pleased with his jeans that he spins his chair about in delight. Another shows a couple in a well-known fast-food chain store using sign language with subtitles for the hearing. A third for a computer company shows a blind and partially paralysed man in the prestigious position of a systems analyst (Disability Now, 1987). It is interesting that in all three, men predominate and only one included a woman. This may be chance or it may be that advertisers believe the general public is not yet ready to accept positive images of women with disabilities.

Social services

The dominant experience of most people with disabilities is of the health service. Although some women in the present study had had contact with social services or social workers, their experience of them ranged from 'dreadful' to 'hopeless' to 'useful' and 'OK'. Experience of voluntary organisations like one woman's contact with the Disabled Living Foundation was reported to be more helpful.

One woman pointed out a consequence of the financial pressures that most public services are facing. The National Health Service is a free service, whereas some social services are means-tested. Although the woman does not feel she has the resources to pay for the care she requires, her community nurses have said that they think she should move over to local authority services. As health services are cut back, more people in her position may be transferred to a service for which they will have to pay. Another consequence of expenditure restraint and the outflow of personnel to the private sector seems to be the high turnover of nursing staff. The same woman talked of the very large number of different people coming into her home each month from the nursing service:

> I suppose on average every month I probably see something like fifty different people. And you've got to be pleasant with them all. There's no question that they are the ones that have to be pleasant. It's me. It's an enormous number. It's a great strain. I find it a strain.

The predominant experience of most women was that the professionals with whom they came into contact regarded the disability as the client's problem. By contrast, the women themselves usually did not feel that disability was an individual problem, even though it has different dimensions for different individuals. To a large extent, they appeared to concur with Oliver (1983), who says that disability is 'a social problem concerned with the effects of a hostile physical and social environment upon impaired individuals'. The individual approach, however, has dominated much professional practice. For instance, a common model in counselling is to view the response to physical disability as akin to bereavement for the lost 'whole' body. While this may be appropriate in some situations, there is a need to distinguish when a problem requires psychotherapy and when it requires practical or material support. The notion of loss is also premised upon an ideal of what the 'whole' or 'complete' body should be.

The dependency and feelings of inferiority which some women with disabilities experience are not so much inherent in their physical condition as conditioned by societal attitudes towards them both as women and as having a disability. These are often promoted by the professional experts with whom they come into contact. The nature of professional practice in medicine and even social work has been to isolate the individual from her social context, especially when the remedial techniques used are based on individual interaction (McKnight, 1981). This also happens through professional definitions of disability which do not reflect consumer need but professional models of treatment. For example, to a doctor the problem may be glaucoma; to a social worker it may be blindness; to the consumer it may be that most traffic lights only have visual signals or that many stairs do not have rails. Professional definitions also tend to give a problem permanence, whereas for the consumer, it may be variable. A woman with a disability may be untroubled in a user-friendly environment one day but severely disabled in a hostile one the next.

The message that is emerging is that professional expertise has been singularly unsuccessful to date in providing support networks for women who are disabled. The reasons for this are complex and possibly relate to the socio-economic status of professional groups in society and their vested interests in providing certain models of care over and above others. The starting point for professional intervention that will be useful for women with disabilities would be to promote their participation in defining their problems and appropriate solutions to them. Social workers need to be prepared to act as a resource to be used by others. Above all is the need to recognise that requiring assistance and support does not imply that a woman is incapable, nor that she needs to be cared for, but is a means of facilitating greater independence and control over her life.

5

Self-image and sexuality

Self-image can be defined as an internal conception of oneself, a significant part of which is made up of body image, i.e. what physical appearance means to people, how they believe they appear to others, and how this influences their behaviour. For many women, self-image is synonymous with body image. The reason for this close link between self-concept and physical appearance is that women are identified socially with their bodies (Edwards, 1987, p. 67).

A woman is taught very early on to be conscious of her body shape, body size, body smell, her hair (including where it should be as well as where it shouldn't be) and her facial features – in short, of her physical appearance. The diet and fashion industry reinforces this concern for much of a woman's life, as a teenager and an adult. The concern is not generally a healthy one. For instance, for most women an interest in diet and weight control is not primarily related to physical fitness and health. It is more of an obsessive preoccupation with appearance and conforming to a norm of attractiveness. Far from improving health, this is often stressful and energy-sapping.

Enormous financial interests are vested in encouraging women to buy certain commodities and services, most of which are geared to changing their physical appearance. Advertising for these products establishes an ideal to which women are encouraged to aspire. In fact, the ideal is elusive because it represents a fantasy, and one that is always changing. But, as such, it effectively ensures a profitable turnover of new clothes, differently styled shoes, hairstyles and all the accoutrements that are supposed to be necessary to reach the goal. For most women with a disability the ideal is difficult, if not impossible, to attain because it implies certain basic features such as being an approximate height or having two ordinarily functioning arms and legs. Even having the aids and instruments to create the ideal may not help. A woman with callipers cannot walk on high heels. A woman with a prosthesis or artificial leg may not feel able to wear a mini-skirt. Make-up is unlikely to transform a woman with facial scarring into a cover girl.

An extension of this is the use of 'attractive' women, i.e. those women who do approximate the ideal, to sell a variety of other commodities such as motor cars and alcoholic drinks, or even newspapers. In the face of this widespread use of women commercially, it is not surprising that women have come to be judged and evaluated according to how they look, by criteria related to external appearances. Nor is it surprising that women have internalised these beliefs about themselves. Even before adulthood girls are taught to admire and strive after prettiness. The fairy stories they read as children encourage this – the pretty Cinderella triumphs over her ugly sisters; Sleeping Beauty is an attractive woman whose beauty is enhanced by her passivity in sleep. Neither is usually portrayed as anything other than a Barbie doll-like creature with long, golden hair, slim waist and elegant limbs. In each case, their beauty is rewarded and their full flowering reached by marriage to a prince, just as the ugliness of Cinderalla's two sisters is punished by the intimation of a lonely life of spinsterhood. The moral of both stories is clear: evil comes in the shape of ugly women, poverty and misshapen witches; good in the shape of pretty women, wealth, princes and physical perfection.

While it is true that both women and men appear in advertising, the significance of physical appearance in women's lives is considerable. For boys and men body image is primarily related to whether their bodies will *do* certain things, whereas for girls and women it is whether their bodies will *look* right and be acceptable (Lawrence, 1987, p. 217). The latter is illustrated by a study in which seventy-five women with orthopaedic disabilities were asked what kinds of activities made them feel more like women. One-third of the women cited activities such as dressing up, wearing make-up, and shopping for clothes. One woman listed 'wearing feminine clothes, taking time with hair and make-up, perfume, delicate jewellery' as important. Another listed 'perfect grooming, becoming clothing, CLEAN! [sic] Clothing in good repair, good hairstyles, careful make-up, outgoing smiles, good dental hygiene, sincere interest in others,' as making her feel more feminine (Duffy, 1981, p. 61).

Women's bodies are linked to their self-image and what they perceive the future has to offer them, although the centrality of body image may vary from woman to woman and may be more significant at different stages of life such as adolescence. A woman's body gives messages to those around her. For instance, Lawrence suggests that 'having the right kind of body provides for women a guarantee of membership of the group of attractive women,' (Lawrence, 1987, p. 211). Conversely, having the 'wrong' kind of body excludes women from that membership, which can be damaging to a women's self-esteem. However, the possibility that it might also be a welcome release from the expectations there are of attractive women, such as sexual availability, should not be overlooked. It can also create a tension between these two responses which some women resolve in extreme and self-harming ways.

Feeling troubled and uneasy about their body inhibits some women from becoming self-respecting, independent and autonomous. In others, it can create more life-threatening symptoms. For instance, anorexia is widely understood as a means of coping with low self-esteem, ironically giving such women a sense of control despite the suffering their actions lead to and the anguish out of which they come (Edwards, 1987). Although the general unease and ambivalence which so many women feel about their body does not always manifest itself so dramatically, it can still inhibit achievement and more positive forms of self-expression.

Physical disability must also be incorporated into one's self-concept. A woman who is born with a physical impairment is likely to be just as influenced by dominant norms and values about attractiveness and physical appearance as any other woman. A woman who becomes disabled is likely to have internalised the dominant values about physical attractiveness. In both situations, the further they perceive themselves to be from the popular standard of beauty, the more likely their self-image, is to suffer.

It does not necessarily follow that disability as such leads to a more negative self-image. In a study of seventy-six disabled and ninety-two non-disabled college students in North America, respondents were asked to rate themselves on a variety of personality traits and attitudes. If was found that a person's gender had a greater impact on their self-perception and self-image than their physical condition (Weinberg-Asher, 1976). This suggests that disabled and non-disabled people are being socialised into similar sex role patterns. In addition, those people in the study with disabilities had a more positive image of themselves than others had of them, suggesting that they do not necessarily appear to be incorporating society's view of disability.

Among a less specific group of women, however, there is some evidence that disability can have an effect on self-image which can be profound and long-lasting. This is partly due to the attitudes of others. Bogle and Shaul (1981) suggest that four things contribute to a negative body image:

1. negative reactions from the outside world (exemplified by statements such as 'she was so pretty before her accident', or expressions of surprise and additional pity at seeing an attractive woman with a disability);
2. lack of control over bodily function which is not usually associated with adulthood;
3. having to incorporate cold, hard, metallic appliances into the concept of warm, soft, lovable femininity;
4. fears of sexual and social rejection.

All these things can lead to self-hatred in which the body become the enemy. Women who are encouraged to become competent and to gain control in other areas of their lives are likely to develop a more positive affirmation of themselves and their bodies.

If a woman becomes disabled, she is obliged to reassess her self-image, and the older she is, the more considerable this process of reassessment is likely to be. Even if she is young, the changes she will experience both in her relationships with others and materially mean that her perception of herself will change. Some women will become even more self-conscious of their bodies. Shantu, a 24-year-old student interviewed for this study said she felt particularly self-conscious when she went swimming – one of the few forms of exercise open to her. An older woman, Enid, reported that when she became a paraplegic, she stopped looking at her legs and still will reveal her body only to her partner of many years' standing. For a number of women, the loss of mobility that disability brings means a sudden stop in exercise and a consequent gain in weight, which can be very distressing. Thomas, in his book *The Experience of Handicap*, quotes a man describing his wife's reaction to having an artificial arm:

> my wife's first response to the accident was not to express concern about her ability to pick up pencils, but to worry if she would still be able to go on a beach in a bikini. Three weeks after the accident, appearance and disguise are her main concerns. (Thomas, 1982, p. 45).

The reassessment is often considerably more complex than simply being related to body image. Nadia, a career woman who developed multiple sclerosis in her late twenties, said:

> You had a new readjustment to make to the fact that you were no longer a working girl, and to the fact that you are ill. Not that you've just suddenly become paralysed and you have to live in a wheelchair – apart from that you're OK and can live till you're seventy. But you've got an illness which is totally uncertain in its nature, so you've no idea whether you can be as good as new. You can drop dead in two years or you can slowly deteriorate. Or you can deteriorate rapidly and be dead in a few years. So what do you do? How do you try and make a life for yourself?

She felt that her disability had not only knocked her self-image but her sense of security:

> You feel yourself insecure as a woman, as well you're insecure as a mother. You feel the dependence of it all, for somebody who is used to independence. I'd started earning and being a big shot. Then suddenly, never mind being a mother and a big shot, you're physically dependent as well. It takes a lot to survive that.

Women who are or become disabled may try to compensate by being better at their work, by maintaining a higher standard of homemaking, by becoming super achievers, by dressing better than either they would have done had they not been disabled or other women would do (Hayslip, 1981). This need to excel does not only come from within themselves but it is a response to high expectations from those around them that they will not complain but will battle on heroically. It appears that women with disabilities are made to feel failures if they don't succeed, and larger than life if they do.

For many women the response to this becomes focused on their standards of dress. Although some recognise the inordinate value that is placed on the physical appearance of women, they nonetheless pay a great deal of attention to the clothes and shoes they wear and often try to look elegant particularly to draw attention away from their impairment. Margaret, who has limited movement in her arms and hands and must wear what she feels is an ungainly prosthesis, expressed her feelings about this:

> I always wear long sleeves. There's no reason why I should in the hot weather. In fact I hate the hot weather, because then I do feel conspicuous. On and off, I've felt it a bit of a pain having to buy or wear the same kinds of clothes. I don't mean flaunting one's sexuality, I don't mean that, but being able to express one's womanliness in that sort of way. Wearing revealing summer clothes and bikinis and things.

Appearance is usually felt to be significantly affected by the use of that largest, most obvious and cumbersome prosthesis, the wheelchair. As one woman very simply put it, 'It's very difficult to be sexy from a wheelchair' (although this presumably refers to a social norm of sexiness that is premised on being able-bodied). The transfer to a wheelchair is often, but not always, traumatic. One young woman expressed a hatred of her chair, another felt that she was more able to look elegant in a chair than in callipers. Becker (1981) suggests out of her own experience that the population at large feels more comfortable with women in wheelchairs than with women who use a stick and callipers, because it fits the stereotype of a helpless, dependent creature. Women themselves, therefore, might come to prefer being in a wheelchair, even though the walking and exercise might be preferable in terms of giving them greater freedom of movement and better for their health.

For some women, it is the clearest and most obvious sign and symbol of their disability, forcing both them and the world to acknowledge a new status. A similar feeling was experienced by Margaret when she was allocated a three-wheeled invalid car. She said:

> In a way that was my equivalent to the wheelchair. It was the first time ever that I'd had something very specific that said, 'You are disabled, you have got the dreaded tricycle to drive.' I think that was very useful in terms of what was going on in the old psyche at the time. It made me come to terms with the disability. And it had got to be faced, really. And by accepting the trike and learning to drive it and using it,

I was having to acknowledge that bit. But it also gave me a level of independence that I'd never had before, which I couldn't have done what I then went on to do, without.

The determining factors of an easy transition seems to be how difficult and dependent life was immediately before the transition, and the balance between the effect of the wheelchair on appearance and the ease of not having to walk. Perhaps it is like most partnerships: there are good times and bad times.

Wheelchairs can be a barrier to communication if for no other reason than they reduce the height of the user, making it easier for standing people to ignore the seated person. On the other hand they can facilitate communication, as in the case of one woman who found that her shyness went away with the advent of her wheelchair and another who had greater concentration in a wheelchair than on crutches. Although there does seem to be a difference in power between users and non-users, the non-user does not always have to have the edge over the user. Debra, extremely successful at working out strategies for coping with people's attitudes to her chair, has reversed the usual balance of power: 'My chair allows me to move fast with people when I want, or at my own pace. I set the controls. There are tricks to learn.' She also insists that people do not clutter up her chair with their handbags or coats, thus forcing others to respect her chair and, therefore, her lifestyle.

Wheelchairs are clearly enabling on one level. Rosemary referred to the 'heavenly relief not to have to keep trying to walk all over the place', and another woman spoke of the pleasure of sitting elegantly rather than stumbling around on what she felt to be unattractive callipers. In her autobiography, Nicole Davoud (1985, p. 40) describes her first encounter with a wheelchair:

Once we went to the Hayward Gallery. A friend had told me that it was possible to reserve a wheelchair in advance. We did – and for the first time since my illness I really enjoyed an outing. The relief at not having to worry about the distance to the nearest chair was indescribable. I could concentrate on the paintings, relax, forget everything else. The wheelchair which had been an object of dread and horror a few months ago, had now become the vehicle through which I could gain the freedom to do the things that I wanted. When the time came to return it, I felt sorry. I wished that I could have taken it home.

Wheelchairs only become disabling in the face of the negative attitudes and behaviour of many non-disabled people. A not uncommon experience is when non-disabled people try to take charge of someone else's wheelchair. This happened to Sheila in the street on day: 'There was this man who came up from behind and pushed me, pushed my chair inside, you know. He just pushed me like I was nothing. Funny what some people think.' Apart from general rudeness, this also expresses an attempt to exert power over, or take control away from, the disabled person.

Sexuality

The expression of sexuality and the participation in sexual relationships is an integral part of self-image and an important means of creating feelings of self-worth. However, just as there are positive ways of expressing sexuality, so there are negative and exploitative ways in which power and control are exerted over people, making them feel worthless. Sexuality in Western society is publicly associated with a standard of attractiveness for both men and women. In men, the standard relates to power and wealth; in women it relates to physical appearance. However, for women, sexuality is usually a complex mixture of being a sexual object and the sexual property of men on the one hand, and having sexual needs in their own right to be expressed either with or independently of men on the other.

One of the most common assumptions made about women with disabilities is that they are asexual (Matthews, 1983, pp. 75, 84; Hayslip, 1981, p. 87). This can be a double-edged sword, because while it exempts them from many sexist assumptions about women, it also excludes them from many things they might wish to be involved in. In other words, it restricts their choices. For instance, when a feminist woman who is disabled decides not to act out the 'feminine' role, her behaviour will not be recognised as a positive act but as part of being disabled. (Campling, 1981a, p. 54). By contrast, other disabled women may wish to opt into an extreme 'feminine' role to overcome the limitations that others impose on their sexual eligibility. The needs of lesbian women are regularly ignored. Rehabilitation staff assume (if they do at all) that women will want to know only about heterosexual sex or birth control, and that women will only play a passive sexual role. Lesbianism, however, is an important option for some women, and it often offers supportive and less threatening relationships than those with men (Bullard and Knight, 1981).

The de-sexing of a woman who is or who becomes disabled takes a number of different forms. Parents do not expect or make provision for dating. Boys and men may either abuse women with disabilities or feel sorry for them. Husbands or lovers are assumed to be brothers and sisters, and children are thought to have been adopted. Ironically, one set of parents' assumptions about their daughter led to her being given greater freedom than her sisters:

> I get a lot of freedom. I go to parties and come home late. And although they worry, they allow it. If my sister wanted to do that it would be out of the question. They think I won't ever get married, or what boy would look at me. I don't know. I'm only guessing. But I think that's what goes on in their minds. So I have more freedom than she has.

However, it is often at adolescence that the limitations our society places on people who are disabled become most acute. It is at this stage of life when young people begin to explore and experiment in relationships and build up a knowledge of the world that they will carry with them into the future. And yet, the ability to participate in this important developmental stage is often severely curtailed for many young people. In a study of 150 teenagers, most of whom were disabled, Anderson and Clarke (1982, p. 88) found that teenagers who were disabled had less experience of dating – girls more so than boys, they had less sexual contact with others, and were less certain they would ultimately get married than non-disabled teenagers. Girls, whether disabled or not, tended to worry more about boyfriends than boys did about girlfriends.

A great many things indirectly affect the building up of relationships and the expression of sexuality. If access into buildings is restricted or if education and employment are either restricted or not integrated, then people with disabilities will not be able to meet other people or to conduct relationships in the way most people expect to be able to. Carole, a nineteen-year-old, spoke of the difficulties of staying out late at night. Not only did the Dial-A-Ride service of public transport for people with disabilities stop at 11.00 pm, but it needed to be booked two weeks in advance, when most teenagers' lives are lived far more spontaneously. The assumption of the service was that most of the disabled users would be elderly. In addition to this, staying out or up late means that a helper needs also to stay up late to assist with pre-bedtime ablutions.

The attitude of men towards women with disabilities is very mixed and complex. Worrying evidence is emerging that some women with disabilities experience sexual abuse such as harassment, molestation, incest and rape. Very little attention has been paid to this by professionals or the public, possibly yet another reflection of the de-sexing of women who are disabled. It has been left to the women themselves to voice their concern and distress (Thurer, 1982). A report from Seattle in the USA recorded over 300 incidents of sexual abuse of women and children with disabilities over a two-and-a half-year period in that one city alone. The study suggests that only 25 – 30 per cent of victims report the abuse. This may be partly due to the fact that 99 per cent of offenders were known to their victims, who were often dependent upon them (Seattle Rape Relief, 1979).

A few women reported being treated in ways they found unhelpful or abusive. One young woman was told by her boyfriend that he had been going out with her because he felt sorry for her and this had been a devastating experience. Another young student felt that the boys in her class tended to be like big brothers protecting her. She became unsure of herself and believed that if anyone was friendly to her or said they liked her, it must be because they felt sorry for her or because they felt good having a disabled friend. Another older woman said she just simply would not show any signs of interest in men, because 'I'm sure they would be rejected. But, anyway, with a body like I've got now, that's the last thing in the world that anybody would want. So, I just forget it.'

Most women are extremely hurt by the assumption that their sexuality has vanished with their being or becoming disabled. They feel very much the imposition of this on their natural feelings and are aware that in some senses they have been put down by this assumption. Felicity said, 'It's bloody hurtful. It's interesting, because men still pay me physical compliments. But they do it knowing they are quite safe.' She felt that as a woman with a disability, she might be less of a threat to other women. However, she also recognises an advantage in this in that she believes she is invited out by married couples more than she would have been as a single, non-disabled woman.

Women who are disabled can also experience the isolation of not having any physical contact outside of the context of medical examinations and treatment (Duffy, 1981, p. 76). People are often afraid to touch other people who are disabled for fear of hurting them. This can be very problematic for sexual relationships, and it can be extremely isolating in ordinary social contacts, as Anita pointed out:

> People have gone out of their way not to have any physical contact with me at all. One of the things when I was very ill, I was on one of these machines and developed a migraine. Five minutes of somebody actually holding my hand or rubbing my forehead, doing something more intimate, would have been worth any amount of aspirins and cold compresses and nobody did. I've been really starved of any sensation. I just think they don't understand my need for any physical contact.

Other women have reported the intrusiveness of carers, therapists and doctors who do not feel they need permission to touch and manipulate the bodies of women who are disabled. In a sense this reflects the same problem of a non-disabled world which has no sense of perspective or boundaries in its contact with disabled women. In both cases women are being treated thoughtlessly and carelessly because their humanity and their sexuality has been denied them.

In contrast to this, some women with disabilities are taking greater trouble to learn more about their sexuality, which frequently leads to greater sexual fulfilment. For instance, having to take greater initiative in sexual relations, experimenting more, using a different and unusual range of sexual positions, and the need for explicit instructions during sexual intercourse are all reported to lead to an enhanced sexual experience (Bullard and Knight, 1981). It is more likely that women with disabilities who are able to overcome an initial shyness or awkwardness will be able to make greater use of their sexual potential.

Marriage

There are also some negative attitudes to disabled women getting married. This may be because marriage is an outward sign of sexuality, but it may also be linked to parents not wishing to give up the child they have protected and nurtured for so long. There is some evidence that mothers' attitudes towards their daughters marrying was very negative. They range from believing that no one would want to marry them, and that no one would want a wife who couldn't take care of the home, to believing that they would only be able to marry a man who was disabled. Margaret encountered a very negative attitude from her parents-in-law:

> The first time I went to my husband's home before we were engaged, the first thing my father-in-law said was 'We never watch medical programmes on the television.' It was quite out of context. It was like saying, we don't like anything medical, we don't want you to come too close. At that time I was just a friend, not a girlfriend. But that was a warning. When we had the statutory tea on Sunday after we were engaged, and it came up about my father having put a notice in the *Telegraph*, my mother-in-law said, 'I don't know what you want to do that for, everybody will know now.'

Fine and Asch (1985) suggest that these attitudes are based on the assumption that women who are disabled will be inappropriate mothers or sexual companions. This type of prejudice makes it difficult for disabled women to reconcile their self-image and identity with traditional concepts of femininity. These feelings of failure and guilt at causing loved ones pain and suffering are not only felt in relation to husbands and partners, but also to other family members, particularly parents (Davoud, 1985, p. 92).

In contrast to these views, the women themselves were generally very positive about marriage, either very much wanting to be married or generally being happy in their existing marriages. Happiness in their marriages did not prevent them from feeling considerable pressure to be good homemakers, not letting their disabilities interfere with their being good wives and mothers. This was often a great strain, as Nadia found when she tried to manage her career, her home and her disability.

> It's infinitely more difficult as a women because you haven't got a nice wife to look after you. A career woman, she hasn't got a wife to come home to. That applies so much more when you're disabled. So, you're very much alone emotionally, you're lacking in the sort of care you need as a disabled person, and if you're a mother, God help you. You have all the guilt and responsibility of bringing up a child. I felt as useful as a mother as a bit of rubbish on the floor. That was heartbreaking.

In the OPCS study of disability in Britain, similar proportions of men and women of working age tended to be married or cohabiting, regardless of sex or disability. Men with disabilities were slightly more likely to be married or cohabiting than either women with disabilities or other men: 68 per cent compared with 64 per cent and 65 per cent. However, among the working-age population, women with disabilities were more likely to be divorced or separated than either men with disabilities or other women: 14 per cent compared with 6 per cent and 7 per cent (Martin and White, 1988, p. 6).

The evidence on marital breakdown and entry into marriage among disabled women has generally been reported to be negative. An early study of 1505 people in Britain with spinal cord injuries (although only 189 of these were women) found higher rates of divorce among the women than the men. Of women who were married at the time of their injury, 7.3 per cent became divorced or separated as against only 4.9 per cent of men. Roughly the same proportion (7 per cent) of women and men who married after injury became divorced. At that time, the percentage of divorces among the general population was about 1 per cent (Guttman, 1964).

A more comprehensive study of 251 people with spinal cord injuries in the USA, compared their marital status with that of the general population in an attempt to test the effect of disability on marriage. It found that their marital status did differ markedly from the general population, but that the difference was even greater for women: 39.1 per cent fewer women married than was expected, and 24.7 per cent more women were divorced or separated than expected (Brown and Giesy, 1986). These studies reinforce much of the qualitative data on marital breakdown such as Bonwich's (1985) study in the United States of thirty-six spinal cord injured women. She found that over half of her respondents reported their marriages or romantic relationships were dissolved after, and because of, their injury.

Although women with disabilities are more vulnerable to desertion than men with disabilities (Franklin, 1977), none of the women interviewed in the present study had experience of this. Nadia, however, felt that disability could be more binding in a marriage, forcing husbands to remain in a marriage they might otherwise have left. She also felt at a disadvantage in marital rows, in not being taken seriously, describing a sense of being 'castrated' when she expressed anger and rage. Similar tensions were found in a study of thirty families in which the mother had a severe hearing loss (Oyer and Paolucci, 1970). Marion, who had not been deserted but was divorced, felt that her disability and her subsequent identification with the disabled community had contributed to the dissolution of her marriage. A study of women with disabilities in the USA found that a major turning point in these women's lives had been not so much in coming to terms with their impairment, but, in doing so, learning to identify with other women who were disabled (Hayslip, 1981, p. 95).

Children

Most girls are encouraged to believe that their main role as women is to bear and raise children, and most go on to do exactly that. However, in the case of girls and women who are disabled, this is curiously lacking, and the option of parenthood is actively discouraged. This is due to many things: a belief that disabled women would not be able to cope, that they are asexual, that the children of disabled parents will suffer, that the disability can be inherited, and that child-rearing requires physical mobility and dexterity. All of these beliefs are false, and the evidence against them abounds. An increasing number of studies have now been done of the needs of mothers with disabilities. The picture presented is not dissimilar to motherhood generally, so long as support systems are available and adjustments are made to the environment where necessary.

Discouragement from bearing children comes from a number of quarters. The medical profession does not have sufficient understanding of the effects of pregnancy and labour on women with physical disabilities, and consequently seems over-cautious about recommending it, although there are notable exceptions. There is also a wide variety of attitudes on the part of health care providers, as one woman's experience of the birth of her now eight-year-old daughter illustrates:

> The first thing the doctor said to me was, 'Have this pregnancy terminated.' I said I didn't want to. Then he said, 'After the pregnancy you can get sterilised'. I said I didn't want to get sterilised. He sent me away for a thinking period. When I went back, he said had I thought about it, and I said I hadn't because I'd already made up my mind. He was very good after that. I found the hospital quite difficult. They didn't know how I was going to deliver the baby with muscular dystrophy. They came up with all sorts of frightening and bewildering ways of how I would deliver

it. I thought, no I don't think so, that doesn't sound like me. They were suggesting suction devices. They said I wouldn't have the muscle to push. Then my doctor said he wasn't sure how I was going to carry out the pregnancy. He said if at about six or seven months they thought it would be too difficult for me, they would take the baby then. I thought, they're planning my life for me. I told them that no way would they take the baby when I was six or seven months. And when I went back to the ante natal, they told me I was to come in about three weeks before the time. So they said they would take me in and start me off. So I said no. And then I went into labour quite naturally and I had her normally. After that, the specialist who looks after my muscular dystrophy said it was amazing, he had never heard of anyone with muscular dystrophy having a baby.

By contrast, this woman's health visitor seems to have been very helpful:

My health visitor was very good, she came in. She taught me how to breathe properly. She was a very aware person. She told me what to expect and what not to expect, and about not panicking. How to breathe if the pain got too much – I found that really helpful. And she explained to my boyfriend what to do. He was there at the birth. He helped me when I forgot how to breathe.

It is clearly legitimate to be concerned about the physical stress that pregnancy might place on a woman who is disabled. But there is cause for concern if that becomes an attempt to put undue pressure on the woman to have an abortion or be sterilised. It is likely to drive women away from formal systems of health care provision which may put them at even greater risk. To some extent attitudes are gradually changing towards both the sexuality of women with disabilities and their rights to motherhood, although most women still need to be quite assertive regarding their needs and wants. The role of policy in encouraging change should not be underestimated. For instance, in the USA many family planning agencies only became concerned with the needs of women with disabilities following an amendment to the 1973 Rehabilitation Act, which stated that no disabled person could be excluded from participation in or benefit from any federally funded programme. This forced many agencies to re-examine their attitudes and make their clinics accessible (Asrael, 1982). It shouldn't be forgotten, however, that the Rehabilitation Act itself only came into force after intensive protests and lobbying by different coalitions of disabled people.

The response of doctors to situations where the disability can be passed on to children also varies. Generally, the perception of having a baby under these circumstances is very different and far more positive on the part of the woman concerned than on the part of the doctor and the rest of society. One woman described her deafness as her family heritage: 'Every time we fall in love and make babies, we pass it on', she says. Another woman with osteogenesis imperfecta described loving her baby with the same condition as 'learning to completely love myself...[rather than]...trying to make up for the mistake of existing' (Mason, 1985). Both women have a very positive self-image, although in one situation a genetic specialist had advised sterilisation.

Families and friends also have a variety of responses to the pregnancy of a woman with a disability. In many cases the reaction is one of delight and enthusiasm. However, in some instances it is one of ambivalence or antagonism. One woman spoke of her brother, who had been so shocked and upset that eight years on, he still had not forgiven her. Another woman's in-laws had been unable to accept it at all, and even after the birth of her little boy spent the whole of his first twelve months saying, 'Poor little mite' whenever they visited.

A number of women expressed concern that their children might be taken into care or that families and friends would interfere in their upbringing. For Audrey this meant the prospect of continually fighting off the interference of well-meaning friends and family:

> I feel that if I do have children, I'm going to have to work extra hard in bringing them up the way I want them to be brought up, because I think people can be very interfering. Well, I can see that happening now. Even sometimes, within this flat, people will come and move things around, you know, and I say, look, forget about that. But I can see bringing up my kids is going to be tough, not because I can't use my hands, but it's going to be tough telling people, look, these are my kids, you've had your share, you can go away and leave me to bring them up.

Some women have had to relinquish the maternal role as a result of disability. Nearly one-third of the women interviewed by Bonwich (1985) who had had children, had given up the custody of their children at the time they became disabled because they could not take care of them. About a half of those who had not yet had children said their disability had forced them to give up their plans to have children – not for medical reasons, but because of financial and physical limitations.

Women with disabilities who do have children develop all sorts of strategies for coping with changing their nappies, bathing them, cuddling or disciplining them and putting them to bed. In many cases this is not difficult, because of the ability of the babies to adapt. One mother who could not use her arms found that her two children both learned to scramble up her and hang around her neck. She also found that they never climbed in and out of their cot, 'But, if I wanted them out of the cot, they'd lean over and hold round my neck, and we'd get them out that way'. With the help of a good occupational therapist she was able to devise a variety of carrying slings and adaptations to such things as nappy fastenings. Another mother taught herself how to change nappies from her wheelchair, sitting alongside her bed. A third woman in a wheelchair, who could not pick up her little boy, would sing to him until he went to sleep. It is not uncommon for women with mobility problems to train their voices to become verbally more assertive and authoritative with their children (Ferris, 1981; Shaul *et al.*, 1985). With flexible attitudes, good ideas and good support services, all these women were able to have their babies and care for them, albeit in unconventional ways.

As children get older, different issues present themselves. Many women mentioned how protective their children were towards them, even at a very young age. They expressed concern about the additional responsibilities their children had to face, although the skills they developed along the way were seen to be a positive outcome of their disability. School-going children have different requirements to babies, and the needs of mothers at this stage of their children's lives often revolve around school. One woman said the most difficult thing was for her to get to see all their teachers. Another talked of the difficulties of living up to the standards of motherhood and dealing with the embarrassment her schoolboy son had at her being in a wheelchair, drawing on her own reserves of emotional strength to do so:

Thank goodness, I am very strong. You know, like going to a prize-giving, and your son is telling you he'd rather you didn't come. That happened when he was about nine or ten. And I understood it. I thought he was ashamed of me. In the end he said he was sort of protecting me. That was the extraordinary thing. So he didn't want me to come because, he said, 'If anybody says anything about you, I'll kill them.' He didn't want to be put in that position in which he had to defend his mother or fight for her.

There is often ambivalence on the part of children, with studies showing similar embarrassments among children, sometimes leading to unco-operative and antagonistic behaviour, and at other times to helpful and supportive actions (Harris, 1986). Overall, however, the children of women who are disabled are often cited as having an increased awareness of other stigmatised groups (Shaul *et al.*, 1972). Nadia felt that her relationship with her son had increasingly got better as he grew older. Having felt guilt and anxiety about her ability to give him sufficient attention as a young child, she had been pleasantly surprised to have him say how much he had valued having her at home more than she might have been had she been an ordinary working mother. It is also possible that her feelings of inadequacy and anxiety are general to most mothers because of the unrealistically high expectations of motherhood that exist in Western society.

The most dominant impression that emerged out of this study and others was that despite discouraging and unhelpful attitudes, most women with disabilities continue to express their sexuality, continue to have the children they want to have, and bring them up no more or less successfully than anyone else.

6

Dependency

Independence is usually taken to mean being able to live with as little reliance on the help of others as possible. It is, therefore, a relative concept. Since human beings are social creatures, it can be said to have no real meaning at its extreme. For women who are disabled and who have very real physical needs which must be met with the help of others, the term becomes even more ambiguous. It is therefore useful to define independence as being able *to determine and take responsibility* for one's life. In the presence of a physical disability this is more than likely to involve relying on help in the form of aids and appliances, housing and workplace adaptations, and personal assistance for day-to-day living. All these things, however, can be provided in different ways. Individuals can be coerced into dependency in return for financial and other forms of help (Scott, 1969; Miller and Gwynne, 1972). Or, they can get help which deliberately promotes or increases autonomy and self-determination (Borsay, 1986; Oliver, 1983). Obstacles to independent living can be both structural and ideological. Physical disability *per se* need not impose a state of dependency on someone, but an unaccommodating and hostile environment or prejudical attitudes will certainly do so. Independence is not only a function of individual abilities, but the interaction between those abilities and the environment – physical and social.

Gender is an important factor in determining whether or not someone is expected or encouraged to be independent. This independence can take many forms, such as making decisions for oneself, living independently, and having the opportunity to earn a living or receiving an adequate income. Women are disadvantaged in all of these, although the 'feminisation' of poverty which accompanies this poverty has only recently begun to be acknowledged and confronted (Glendinning and Millar, 1987). For women, the status of 'disabled' compounds their status of being 'female' to create a unique type of oppression (Croxon John, 1988). Female children are defined by their gender and taught to behave in gender-specific ways such as being less active and assertive than male children. Women who are born disabled or who become disabled at a very early age find that they are defined predominantly by their physical condition. They are given less responsibility and are often taught to be helpless. Things are done for and to them. While this process is quite natural for infants and children, it often continues into adolescence and adult life for women with disabilities. At best, this process of infantilisation provides comfort, love and help. However, it also prevents independence and, at worst, depersonalises people.

Women who become disabled at an older age find that they have their adult status removed and are relegated to that of childhood, with its concomitant loss of control, decision-making and opportunity to live independently. Because the female sex role is predominantly a passive one, it has been suggested that becoming disabled for a woman is less significant than it is for a man, who loses the dignity of being active and taking responsibility for his life (Campling, 1981a, p. 119). This neglects the significant amount of responsibility that women often bear in combining two jobs – one paid and the other running a home and rearing children. There is increasing evidence that the portrayal of women as passive is at an ideological level and is to some extent out of touch with their real lives or desires. The issues that confront women who are or become disabled are different to those that confront men, but there is no evidence that they are less problematic. The evidence suggests that, if anything, they are sometimes more problematic on an interpersonal as well as a material level (Deegan and Brooks, 1985).

Women who are disabled face the threat of psychological, physical and material dependency. In a number of ways they are prevented from making decisions about things that crucially affect their lives. They are often dependent on parents long after the age when most young women would expect to leave the parental home. For some, the lack of appropriate living accommodation means life in residential accommodation where the rules and rigours of institutional life mean the loss of privacy and basic freedoms of choice (Hannaford, 1985).

Women who have left their childhood home and who do not live in an institution may still find themselves dependent on husbands, although compared to other women, women with disabilities are more likely not to marry, to marry at a later age, or to be divorced (Franklin, 1977; Sainsbury, 1970; Topliss, 1979; Kutza, 1981; Brown and Giesy, 1986). The nature of a woman's dependency on her spouse is complex and lies in the roles and duties which women are expected to perform (which may also explain the higher incidence of single or divorced statuses among women with disabilities). They are simultaneously expected to be sexual playthings, responsive and caring companions and good mothers. When a woman marries, she becomes part of her husband's domain. She takes his name and becomes his dependant both symbolically and often materially. Her behaviour and actions will reflect on him and his family name. She is perceived either to enhance or demean his status in the world.

Physical disability represents a threat to these expectations and this role. One woman who became disabled two years after getting married describes her feelings of guilt and failure thus: 'It took me a long time to stop (mentally) apologising to my husband for existing, and to stop regarding him, as others around me did, as something of a saint because he did *not* leave me,' (Campling, 1981a, p. 40). She felt this was due to the role she as a woman was expected to fulfil in enhancing her husband's position among his peers. Two aspects of this role – being an adequate sexual partner and being able to undertake the servicing tasks expected of a wife – have particular consequences for someone who is disabled.

Dependency is most commonly reported as being overprotected, especially in the parental home, but also in the marital home: having one's privacy invaded at home particularly by health care professionals; and not being allowed to make decisions.

The parental home

Many women who are disabled stay in the parental home long beyond the time that is normal for most young women in Western society, into their late twenties and thirties. During this time most of the daily care and attention they receive comes from their mothers. Sometimes this creates an intense bond between the two women and at other times it can cause conflict. In many situations there is an ambivalence on both sides. Many women recognise that without the considerable help available to them from their mothers, they would have spent their childhood in residential care. And yet they see no reason why they should feel grateful for assistance that for them is simply a necessary part of being able to live, or, as they see it, their human right.

The parental home is an environment which can be both helpful and exasperating. It is helpful because there is no need continually to explain one's needs. Both Swasti and Shantu felt their extended families provided company and meant they were never lonely:

> I think I'm happy living with my family, not because I'm disabled, just generally. I'm happy surrounded by people. I hate the thought of being on my own. Not because of all the problems I'll face, not that, it's just that I need company.

> I'm very much a company person. I don't like being by myself. I wouldn't like a flat on my own, it doesn't appeal. Being disabled or not, I'm just not into it. I like people.

They experienced their family homes as joyful places even though they recognised that one day they would want to make their own way. This was also the feeling of a thirty-year-old woman still living with her mother and brothers and sisters and feeling happy about doing so. A common factor in all three situations seemed to be the presence of strong, extended families or a strong community. One of the women said she lived in a very supportive black community which was always available to help and provide her with company. Nonetheless, all the women still living at home felt overprotected to some extent.

An older woman said that in retrospect she felt that her parental home had inhibited her from meeting other young people, especially of the opposite sex. It had limited her socially to the extent that she found it difficult to hold a conversation and developed an inferiority complex. She had very unhappy memories of that time which had in fact constituted virtually half her life to date, i.e. thirty years. Her real break with that environment came when she managed to get an outside job. Another woman, also unhappy at home, found her life there extremely restrictive, with a father she describes as a 'psychological bully' who looked after her out of duty not love. She commented on the additional difficulties she had had as a lesbian woman in bringing her partners home.

A number of women in such situations or wanting to live independently have found that one of the means of moving away from the parental home has been to go into residential care or sheltered accommodation as a stepping stone to having their own home. None remembered this time as pleasant, but most saw it as a necessary intermediate step to independent living. The transition out of their parental homes was also difficult and traumatic. It was something most parents found difficult to accept, as did Anita's:

> Of course, my mother was thoroughly upset. I think she felt that nobody would be able to care for me that much and that's very common – if you talk to people now, that's a very common main expression. And it's true basically. But I was determined to go. I was absolutely determined that we would never get in this muddle. She could never have a day off sick. Simply awful really. So, after much heart searching and dithering, I did go [into residential care].

Living independently

Having made the decision and getting through the break with parents comes the reality of life on one's own. This initially can be isolating and lonely, but it is more often challenging and empowering. A number of women described the mixture of fear and exhilaration they felt on their first night alone.

> It was just like receiving a very long cold shower. It was dreadful. I sat in this room. I'd achieved getting a room of my own and having to make my own decisions. But actually, I'd never made any. I'd made the decision to move but I felt very, very immature. I mean, I realised it myself. I sat in the room by myself. The first evening I will never ever forget. When the door shut behind me, I felt completely alone. I think it was the first time at 29 that I'd ever felt alone and that was a very odd feeling. Because, you know, you're often very public when you're disabled. I almost felt that first sensation of a little power. In a way. But I sat in this room and had never switched on an appliance before, had never made a cup of tea, you know.

Anita felt her dependency had been fostered by too much care and protection, both physically and emotionally. Not only had she not made tea or washed her clothes before, but she had also been stifled emotionally. She remembers not having even made a conscious decision about what to wear up to that point in her life, nor having been allowed to feel fear or pain or frustration. For her, living independently meant a new start: 'It was like a new beginning really, because I'd never actually begun'.

Shearer's (1982) study of six families living independently also notes the excitement of one woman at discovering she could cope with some quite daunting experiences, such as a power cut leaving her stranded in mid air on her hoist. Audrey, who has no use of her arms but feet and legs which function excellently, also had a rather dramatic experience on her first night alone:

> My first night here when I moved was a Sunday. Oh, it was funny. I was using my manual chair and I fell out of my chair. Oh! It was such a shock because I didn't have anyone here. It was my first night here, my completely first night living alone in a flat by myself! And I just remember just crying, you know. You fool! Why did you leave home? And then I thought, well, look you've got to stop crying because you put yourself in this mess and you've got to get yourself out of this mess. So I rang the ambulance. I could wriggle and once I got there, I rang them and said, look, this is what's happened. So they said, yes, we'll come along. It took them about two and a half hours before they came. I had to prop myself by the main door, so that if they rang the intercom, I would be there.

Of course, crucial to anyone's ability to live independently is having suitable accommodation that is provided or having the financial means to provide it for oneself. The former is probably a more realistic option given the relatively poorer circumstances of most people who are disabled (as outlined in the following chapters), but present provision has its own peculiar pitfalls. Two young girls each living with their families had experienced a difficult dilemma. Both had been housed with their families, one in a ground floor Housing Trust property, the other in a council bungalow. Both properties had been substantially adapted and made accessible for the two young women, but both were large family houses. They had reached an age when they would have liked to leave home and live independently, one being nineteen, the other twenty-three. Their dilemma was that whatever they did – stay in their present adapted home or move to another, smaller adapted home – their need for independence meant their parents would have to be rehoused. No longer having a disabled member of the family would mean that the parents would lose their priority for assisted housing.

If I moved on my own, the possibility is that my parents would have to leave here. If they were to move from here and leave me here, I don't know what I'd do with a five-bedroomed house. It's too big. So, it's a Catch 22 situation. It's awkward, because if I want to leave, I really have to think about it. It could lead to a lot of conflict in the house.

In this situation, public housing had given both women greater independence by providing them with accessible and convenient accommodation, while at the same time imprisoning them into a dependency on their families. In addition, both had experienced resistance from their mothers to the idea of their living alone. The predicament they found themselves in was an extremely difficult one for a young person to resolve. One expressed a strong wish to discuss her dilemma with a social worker but felt that her mother would not approve if she did.

Such difficulties are compounded by the scarcity of housing and support services throughout Britain. One study has found that only 10 per cent of housing authorities, 30 per cent of social services departments, and 20 per cent of district health authorities were making any sort of provision for people with severe disabilities. What housing provision there was, consisted largely of warden-assisted sheltered housing or policies on adaptations aside from residential homes. Provision was generally found to be inadequate and planning non-existent (Fiedler, 1988).

Over half of physically disabled adults under retirement age are in inappropriate accommodation such as geriatric hospital wards and old people's homes in the local authority, voluntary and private sectors, (Royal College of Physicians, 1986a, p. 9). A report by Shelter refers to this as part of the problem of 'hidden housing' in which people with disabilities, while not actually homeless, are unable to leave such places due to lack of alternative appropriate provision and services. Similar forms of such 'hidden housing' are when people with disabilities are unable to leave the parental home or are imprisoned in inaccessible buildings (Shelter, 1988, p. 6).

There was a time when the placement of younger people with disabilities into largely geriatric wards was recognised as inappropriate. In the 1970 Chronically Sick and Disabled Person's Bill that came before Parliament, a clause proposed to make this unlawful. However, it was removed from the final Act, and Sections 17 and 18 of that Act now simply discourage such practice – in the public sphere, at least. The private sector appears to be exempt from such constraints (Royal College of Physicians, 1986a, p. 6).

The private rented sector contributes least to the provision of housing for people with disabilities, while the public rented sector makes the greatest contribution. However, the 1980s saw the expansion and deregulation (from rent control) of the private rented sector, while the public sector was broken up and reduced over the same period, (Royal College of Physicians, 1986a, p. 12). Both trends have been the result of deliberate government social policy over the period, and both trends will severely affect people with physical disabilities who are looking for adapted or special housing. The private rented sector is an important source of housing for single women, most of whom are elderly and who are, therefore, likely to include a high proportion of disabled women (Shelter, 1988, p. 12). It is also an important source of housing for young people starting out in life. A deregulated housing market will make it expensive and difficult for such low-income groups, and virtually impossible for young disabled adults wishing to leave the parental home.

Housing tenure often reflects inequalities in income between different groups. People with disabilities are less likely to be owner-occupiers, with only 46 per cent owning their homes as against 59 per cent of the general population. More people of working age who are disabled are likely to be renters than owner-occupiers (Martin and White, 1988). Housing tenure also reflects inequalities between men and women, with women being under-represented in the most desirable tenures: for example 80 per cent of owner-occupied households are headed by men, compared with 69 per cent of council houses (Ginsburg, 1983). It is probable that this pattern is reflected among the population of people with disabilities.

Feelings of dependency are also experienced in the marital home. One woman compared her husband's need to be needed to the feelings of parents about their children. She was irritated by his inability to let her be independent and his problems over letting her go. Similarly, another woman felt that as she became more independent and able to run her own life, she and her husband started drifting apart. She started to identify more and more with other people who were disabled and they eventually separated, with the result that she felt happier and more contented with her new identity. By contrast, another woman expressed enormous anger and resentment against her husband at the inequality which she felt her dependency on him had introduced into their marriage.

Privacy

As one woman said, 'you're often very public when you're disabled'. Although the need for privacy varies from person to person, the less one has of it, the greater is one's need for it. Privacy is very often a rare and precious thing for someone who is disabled. Many women's first experience of their privacy being invaded was in relation to their bodies and health care. Medical examinations are often undertaken by groups of male doctors, who, despite their white coats, can still be perceived by their women patients as simply groups of anonymous men. The treatment of many disabled women by health care staff appears to be impersonal and dehumanising, as some of these accounts indicate.

> About every three months and then every six months, I trailed to the hospital . . . We used to have to wait hours. I hated going, and I had to stand there in my vest and knickers, and there were usually students. And they always used to ask the same questions.

> It's hard to describe. I had to have things like a catheter done – manual evacuation of the faeces. People whipped the bedclothes off you, loads of people round your bed you don't know, and you can't even cover your face up. That was appalling. The only way I could cope was to switch off, and to become incommunicado, as it were.

In some instances this kind of public display or questioning seemed entirely unnecessary. At a very sensitive age as a teenager, Alicia was asked to walk without clothes in front of a number of medical students. The reasons for this were never explained to her, nor could she understand it as having had any relevance to her having cerebral palsy:

> I remember when I was twelve or thirteen, I was asked to parade up and down the best way I could, naked, in front of all these male students. Just coming to puberty. I was so humiliated . . . I couldn't walk anyway, there was no point in trying to make me struggle. They have no feeling whatsoever for you at all.

Enid was asked extremely personal questions, again with little explanation of their relevance to the treatment of her paraplegia. She felt that the questions had been voyeuristic, insensitive and unnecessary:

> This doctor was giving me a gynaecological examination. I was in the public wards then as an ordinary patient and there were all these screens, but everyone could hear what was being said. He said, 'How much sexual sensation do you have?' Everyone could hear! I said, 'none at all!' I thought that was the limit. He didn't say why he asked me. I would just not answer the question.

A number of women have said they object as much to the invasion of their privacy as to the failure of others to recognise that they should have control over their bodies and what happens to them. Anita felt this very strongly:

> Over the years . . . not the *slightest* thought has ever been given to how I felt about men taking photographs of me naked . . . um . . . and doing much more intimate things for me, because you know, males have now come into hospitals, at least as nurses. I don't actually particularly mind that . . . But I think the whole issue is that you're not actually asked.

Jule felt that she too had been denied both privacy and the freedom to say no to certain behaviour:

> Into the room marched a series of different medics, an auxiliary who wasn't busy and thought she had time to see this assessment, with me on the bed being pulled in all directions, with a consultant and his shorthand typist. That is a negation of your own dignity. In that situation, it's harder for a women to say, 'I don't like this, will you tell the rest of the staff to go.' A man might be heard in those circumstances, but for a woman it's very hard.

Miller and Gwynne (1972) documented a similar experience they had as non-medical researchers, when they were invited to examine the body of a woman suffering from arthritis, without her permission being asked and for no real purpose. These sorts of incidents were related by women of all ages, indicating that this sort of practice in hospitals is not simply something which can be brushed aside as belonging to the bad old days when no-one knew any better. Swasti, who is only twenty-three, still experiences it. However, despite the fact that as a young woman she has been placed into a vulnerable and powerless position in front of a group of her peers, she has defined the problem as being due to her own shyness and inhibitions:

> I think there should be more women consultants. I'm pretty shy when it comes to my body, and I think doctors are very ruthless, and they let you sit there with no clothes on while they talk to their students. There's always students at the hospital. You feel so embarrassed. And they just talk in their own gabble. I don't like that, but I'm a bit inhibited.

The invasion of privacy is something that also happens in schools and residential institutions. Many women experience this in relation to menstruation. For example, a woman who attended a residential school, said:

> I wanted privacy, especially when I first started having periods. I was fifteen and the youngest was six. You got washed in front of all of them. And you had your period pads changed in front of them. I learned about periods and that from what I had seen when I was younger.

Other women also report problems with menstruation, especially women who are paralysed and cannot insert their own tampons or apply sanitary towels. If there is no sensation in the vaginal area, a sudden onset of bleeding can cause embarrassing and inconvenient stains, especially during menopause when bleeding may be particularly heavy (Campling, 1981a, p. 125). How different this would be if we celebrated menstruation in our society as a sign of adulthood, fecundity and creativity rather than a taboo. A North American study found a lack of sympathy on the part of consultants towards menstrual cycle problems brought about or increased by disability or its treatment, as in dialysis therapy (Kutner and Gray, 1981).

By contrast, Sheila, who has lived in residential care for most of her life, said that after her initial embarrassment at male care staff changing her sanitary towels, she had decided that she would not let it bother her as it was a natural function. She found the lack of basic privacy and lack of control more of a problem than the embarrassment of others having to perform such intimate tasks for her. This may have been because issues such as menstruation and toileting present themselves more as tiresome, practical problems which some women do not want to let become a hindrance to a more outgoing life. They certainly seem to be experienced as such by women in wheelchairs, who expressed greater concern over odours, leakages or thrush than mortification at being helped by others. As with all women, the meaning attached to menstruation influences the extent to which it is perceived to be causing dependency.

An extreme lack of privacy was experienced by Debra, who went into sheltered accommodation en route to living independently. Coming from a home where she had had some privacy, she found other residents very invasive and put it down to their being institutionalised. Nevertheless, she felt willing to put up with a decline in privacy for her greater goal of living independently. People whose disabilities make their health more vulnerable are possibly likely to have even less privacy. One woman mentioned that she was not supposed to be left alone for any length of time in case she suddenly went into crisis. What offended her sense of dignity most, however, was not even being able to keep details of her bank account private, as she was unable to get into her bank because the building was inaccessible to wheelchairs.

Concern was also expressed about a lack of privacy generally. Women living with parents and families spoke of people coming into their rooms without knocking, and using their things without permission. Other women spoke of having an extreme need for privacy because of the total lack of it when they were growing up. One woman said she felt physically sick when her community nurses overstepped the boundaries she had drawn for them in her flat. Lack of privacy for her, as for others, felt demeaning – as if she was losing control over her life.

Decision-making and control

A great many women talked about the way a disability could cause loss of control over their lives. They felt this had happened in a number of different areas – within their families, at school, at work and in contact with professionals and the general public. A few women expressed a desire to be able to contribute to food and household costs. Others said they wished people would ask more of them but they had noticed that people rarely asked favours of them, which is another way of reinforcing an inferior, dependent status.

The education we all get is crucial in determining our life's chances and our ability to be independent. School is where we first start to broaden our horizons beyond that of the parental home, and where we come under the powerful influence of our peers. Prior to the 1981 Education Act, children with disabilities could attend ordinary schools only with great difficulty, and usually only if they had ambitious and determined parents. At such schools they were usually in a minority of one. While getting an education equal to that of their peers, they nonetheless suffered the lack of strong role models in teachers. Most children with disabilities, however, attended (and still do) special schools, where they are not only segregated from the majority, but socialised into a lesser, minority status.

Women who had attended special schools said they felt their education had been far from adequate, with undue emphasis being placed on medical care and training in living skills at the expense of getting a good academic education. This emphasis was built into the very structure of special education prior to 1970, when responsibility for the education of children with severe disabilities came under the Department of Health and Social Security rather than where it more properly should have been in the Department of Education and Science.

> If you're going to be disturbed from your Maths class to go to physiotherapy, that's wrong. Physiotherapy and hydrotherapy should be a separate thing from school. It shouldn't affect your education. So, you're disabled – surely you should try to come out as an intelligent person. It's bad enough being disabled, but to have no qualifications either, then you're going into the world of work with nothing.

Even though many special schools seem to emphasise training in practical skills, according to Bookis (1983), some women felt they were lacking even in these when they left school. One young nineteen-year-old felt that her independence training at school had not even equipped her to budget her money. The training seems to be oriented towards coping with the disability rather than coping with living independently:

> I learned to get myself on and off the loo, you know, things like that. But I never really learned anything. With all the things they said they could offer me, in the end, there was nothing.'

Although the 1981 Education Act made provision for children with disabilities to be integrated into ordinary schools, it did not make extra resources available to facilitate this, in contrast to the United States where federal funding financed the costs of adapting ordinary schools and their curricula (Shearer, 1981a, p. 47). Some local authorities, such as the Inner London Education Authority (ILEA), moved swiftly towards greater integration, while others did not. In the case of ILEA, this was sometimes in the face of strong opposition from parents who feared that the special needs of their children would be neglected in an ordinary school environment. Other parents, however, agreed that that their children's academic needs would best be met alongside non-disabled children, who at the same time would learn not to be prejudiced against people who were physically different. The goal of integration was to 'make ordinary schools special enough to meet the needs of children with disabilities', and to teach the other children to be tolerant of difference (Shearer, 1981a, p. 50).

Not being given a proper education not only implies a life of dependency, but ensures that women leaving school will not be equipped to earn a living and will lack the confidence to make their way in the world. A poor or negligible education is the most effective means of denying individuals the same life chances as anyone else. Special schools often seem to encourage dependency and are as overprotective as some parents. One young woman described the contrast between being at her special school and being at an ordinary college:

> There was hardly anybody disabled when I went – it hits you, very hard. You're suddenly there, and you find out things you never even dreamt of. When you went to the special school, the bus picks you up from your front door, takes you to the school, puts you inside the building, then picks you up and drops you off home. That was your world. And this was totally different.

Few women were able to attend universities or colleges of higher education, but those that did had usually gone to an ordinary school due to the extremely high motivation of their parents to get them into ordinary schools. Usually they had been the only disabled child in their class, which had presented its own pressures in terms of having to compete. One woman said she felt this had been good and had driven her to achieve things, although it also made her have overly high expectations of herself which she was only getting into perspective in her mid thirties.

A problem in higher education that was mentioned a few times was the difficulty in using libraries and the dependency on fellow students which this led to. One young woman in a wheelchair was unable to get to a library which was inaccessible. As a law student, the solution that was devised to this problem, writing down the books she needed and giving it to the librarian, was unsuitable, and as might be expected, she did not pass. Her ability to understand law was not being tested, but her ability to get to a library was. Another woman with limited use of her arms and hands also faced this problem.

> One thing I never got sorted out was the whole business with the library. And the books – not finding it easy to get books off shelves. It was a bind. You either had to have somebody trailing along getting bored, or you had to hope that you hit the right book the first time. The mechanics of getting it back on the shelf was too much.

Many women found the involvement of professionals in their life hampered them. They are put into a passive position when they become disabled, lose what independence they had, and their adult status, returns to that of childhood with its concomitant loss of control, decision-making and autonomy. The organisations and institutions with which they come into contact often perpetuate this dependency (Scott, 1970). Most significantly, they fall into the orbit of the professional or the rehabilitation 'expert' who, more often than not, perpetuates an existing stereotype of what it is to have a disability. It is not unusual for a woman with a disability to be labelled unrealistic when she attempts to live independently, especially if her plans do not conform to the expected female role (Safilios-Rothschild, 1977, p. 40).

> I think the thing was to understand the horror of always being at the mercy of professionals, that no longer had you any control over your own life. It wasn't just a question that you couldn't walk or you couldn't see or hear, or whatever your disability was. It was the fact that you couldn't actually do anything in your life without some professional coming along and controlling that. A professional telling you what sort of wheelchair to have, a professional to tell you how to revamp your house, professionals to tell you what welfare rights you had. For an adult, it is a very extraordinary experience. Added to that was the gratitude that you got any help at all. And how did you balance the gratitude with the anger at having to always ask.

Bookis's (1983) study of disabled school-leavers also found that professionals in the field of careers advice had had a minimal impact on the young people counselled, who had not found the advice received relevant. Similarly, Blaxter (1976, p. 180) found that professionals and formal agencies were of little help in solving the employment problems of people with disabilities. Out of these feelings has come the desire for people who are disabled to wrest control of their lives back from the professionals, to come together for mutual support and self-help. This means not only deciding for themselves as individuals how to live their lives but joining together with other disabled people to organise together to arrive at the most effective ways of doing so. One woman suggested there was an urgent need for women with disabilities to have positive role models, but that this would only come about once disabled people had a say over their own lives.

> In so far as women with disabilities have become more organised, disability has become more organised politically. I think the control we have over policy issues, the control, we have over presenting our own resource material, our own media, videos and everything, could take a while, but generally those sorts of models will be presented so that people will have a greater sense of strength in terms of what their own potential can be. I think the more we are able to get into those positions, the more supportive we can be to other people. That's why we should be in control of policy areas. I'm very positive about what women with disabilities can achieve.

Other women talked about the need for assertiveness training to overcome some of the inhibitions they felt. Sheila had attended just such a course and felt it had successfully changed her manner and behaviour towards others. Another woman felt the need for independence training. However, a number of women also pointed to their need for very practical help like transport, adapted toilets, care assistants, and so on, without which other forms of independence were simply non-starters. However, the lack of such practical assistance and the lack of accessibility reflects not only society's lack of concern and respect for the rights of all individuals regardless of their physical ability, but also the fact that disabled people are not involved in the processes of decision-making which ultimately determine what is and what is not provided.

In recent years, the disabled persons movement has campaigned strongly for recognition of the right to be independent. Probably the most significant development has been the establishment of Centres for Independent Living in the United States and Britain. The centres use the first-hand experience of people with disabilities to provide a comprehensive range of services to assist people to lead an independent and integrated life (Derbyshire Coalition of Disabled People, 1985). A guiding principle is that the centres should be controlled by people with disabilities. This is not always acceptable by funding bodies, but it is a critical premise in the philosophy of Centres for Independent Living. While each Centre may develop its own character, they essentially provide information, advice and services by people with disabilities for people with disabilities. This philosophy is increasingly being seen by many people with disabilities as an important step in the road to overcoming dependency.

7

Employment

Independence is only possible when individuals have an adequate income or material base from which to proceed. In industrial society this comes primarily from employment, except when the state provides a replacement for income through the social security system or when individuals have access to income generating assets. In all three cases, women are often at a disadvantage, as are people with disabilities (Glendinning and Millar, 1987; Disability Alliance, 1987).

Aside from generating an income, employment also structures the day and provides interests, friendships and gives a certain pace to life. The loss of a job and consequent unemployment, or the inability to take on paid work due to disability, can therefore mean not only material hardship but also loneliness, boredom, loss of confidence, and the problem of having surplus unstructured time. These effects have been found among women as much as among men (Coyle, 1984). People with disabilities are at a serious disadvantage compared to the rest of the population in the labour market. They are less likely to have paid work. Thirty-three per cent of men with disabilities and 29 per cent of women with disabilities are in paid work, compared to 78 per cent of men and 60 per cent of women generally. They tend to work in lower-status, lower-paid jobs. Consequently, their income from employment is less than that of other people. They also have a greater propensity for unemployment. Their economic status as a whole, therefore, is lower than that of others. This is exacerbated if they are women. Higher proportions of women with disabilities are in unskilled work than both men with disabilities and non-disabled women, as illustrated in Table 7.1.

Table 7.1 *Socio-economic status of men and women under pension age according to sex and whether disabled or not (%)*

Socio-economic group	Disabled		Non-disabled	
	Male	Female	Male	Female
Professional	3	1	8	1
Employer/managerial	15	6	20	8
Intermediate non-manual	9	16	10	20
Junior non-manual	10	28	8	34
Skilled manual and own account non-professional	37	12	37	8
Semi-skilled manual and personal service	19	26	14	23
Unskilled	7	11	4	6

Source: Martin *et al.* (1989) *Disabled Adults: Services Transport and Employment*, Table 7.20.

In the United States, the same low proportion of women with disabilities were found to be in paid work, i.e. 29 per cent, although a much higher proportion of men were, i.e. 60 per cent (Levitan and Taggart, 1977). Again, both were much lower proportions than in the general population. The men also had higher average weekly earnings. Regular surveys of disability undertaken by the Social Security Administration in the United States show that while *all* people with disabilities are less likely to be employed, both disabled and non-disabled women are even less likely to be than their male counterparts. Marked male/female differentials exist in both groups (Kutner, 1984). This is partly due to women being less likely to return to employment after the onset of disability. One study found 44 per cent of women returning to work, compared to 70 per cent of men (Thurer, 1982). In addition to the male/female differences, there are also differences related to class and race among women with disabilities themselves. Kutner and Gray (1981) found that black women on dialysis tended to give up work more frequently than white women on dialysis. This was thought to be due to socio-economic differences between the two groups and their access to jobs in the labour market.

Work on the effects of disability on employment has rarely focused specifically on women. Campling (1979) first aired some of the employment issues confronting women with disabilities in Britain. Perry (1984) interviewed forty-two women with disabilities in South London, of all ages and varying backgrounds and races. A small and exploratory study, it is rich in insights about the effect that being both female and disabled has on employment opportunities. Most of the women interviewed saw employment as a passport to independence, which was predominantly perceived as having money and control over income. In addition to this, Davoud (1980) has looked at the availability and possibility of part-time work, given the restrictive rules surrounding the receipt of social security benefits. There has also been some work on the development of homeworking schemes for people with disabilities (Ashok *et al.*, 1985; NACEDP, 1983). None of the latter three studies focused on women, but all have particular relevance to women, given their predominance in part-time work and home-working.

Other studies, while also not focusing on women, have looked at the effect of specific disabilities on employment such as multiple sclerosis, which has a particularly high incidence among women (Davoud and Kettle, 1980; Mitchell, 1981; Zeldow and Pavlou, 1984) or have had samples consisting mainly of women (Hopper, 1981). In North America, greater consideration seems to have been given to the issue, and many more studies of employment and disability take account of women's experience. A number of studies have found a positive association between employment and the health of women generally (Nathanson, 1980; Jennings *et al.*, 1984; Passanante and Nathanson, 1985), even when controlling for the possibility that unhealthy women leave employment (Anson and Anson, 1986). In other words, women in paid employment appear to be in better states of health, both mentally and physically. The exclusion of women with disabilities from the labour market, therefore, may worsen their health as well as their material well-being.

The search for jobs

One explanation for the lack of research or research interest in women with disabilities and employment might be the belief that women are less likely to be, or want to be, in paid employment. There is a common assumption that the typical worker is male, able-bodied and available for work at set hours of the day. This stereotyped belief that women's place is primarily in the home is even more likely to lead to the view that women who are or become disabled will more readily and easily withdraw from the labour market than men. One women in the present study felt that when it came to women there was an 'assumed image of disability [which] is about sitting at home, not being able to do anything'. Blaxter's study (1976, p. 156) found that doctors were more inclined to suggest to women than men that they stay home a bit after the onset of disability, and the predisposition of the rehabilitation services towards assisting men rather than women to return to employment has already been discussed in Chapter 4. Clearly, many services also make this assumption, as was indicated in the lack of proper educational provision which is available in some special schools. Consequently, it is difficult for a woman with a disability to obtain paid work, but there is no evidence that this is voluntary.

A number of women do voluntary unpaid work either as a stepping stone to getting employment or as an alternative when they cannot get it. The reasons they find it difficult to get employment are many. Sometimes, they face outright discrimination, as in the case of Alicia, who has cerebral palsy:

> One of the careers officers knew I was unemployed, so she came to see me and said would I be interested in this receptionist job. So I had an interview and then they rung and said I hadn't got it. A couple of weeks after that I found out why I didn't get it. It was because two people on the interview panel said because I was disabled, I would frighten the clients. They said they wouldn't be able to cope with someone who was disabled.

At other times women with disabilities face structural barriers, as did Jule, who walks with a stick due to childhood polio:

> I left school at eighteen with A levels. I was quite interested in library work, but that was a non-starter because I was told I wouldn't be able to cope with the physical nature of the job. They weren't prepared to make structural changes.

This seems to be a common experience: women are *told* they cannot cope rather than being *asked* whether they can. It also not so subtly locates the problem within the woman with the disability rather than in the environment in which they wish to work. A qualified lawyer in the study found it so difficult to get a job that was not below her level of qualification that she eventually applied for one on the community programme for the long-term unemployed. When at last she was offered a reasonable job, she was turned down on the medical grounds when they discovered she had some difficulty walking and needed to use a stick. This left her depressed and upset, having had her hopes raised and then not fulfilled.

Given that women with A levels and professional qualifications find it difficult to get jobs, it is likely to be much more difficult for those women who were not given a proper education to begin with. Some women have spoken about the stigma of being disabled job-seekers, about the lack of choice they have, and how these problems become exacerbated for them when they are also confronted with racism. All the black women interviewed in this study nonetheless felt that despite the considerable racism they encountered, their greatest hurdle in looking for employment had been their physical disability rather than their sex or their race.

One woman faced an extraordinary case of alleged discrimination when, as a deaf person, she applied to two colleges to become a teacher of deaf people and was turned down. Ironically, she went on to become a successful journalist and role model for the pupils she had not been able to teach. A 1987 study by the Royal National Institute for the Deaf points to the small number of deaf staff employed in schools for the deaf. They suggest that this fails to offer deaf children positive role models and the opportunity to come into contact with successfully employed adults who are also deaf. Another woman with cerebral palsy who was in paid work had experienced the prejudice that comes out of ignorance from a boss who did not understand that she had problems in her sense of direction and perception. Although this was in an organisation operating in the field of disability, it is possible that some traditional disability organisations have very entrenched sets of values about the rights of people with disabilities to independence. Most women apply for a large number and variety of jobs, but are turned down. Many felt that there were not enough disabled people or women in high positions in the labour force. This could obviously be a reason why they are not given fair treatment when applying for jobs, since they are not being judged by people whose perceptions of them might be less prejudiced.

Because of all the barriers that exist when women who are disabled wish to find employment, they may find they have to travel much further afield than most to get appropriate jobs. One woman said she specifically looked for work in certain local authorities which had progressive policies towards people with disabilities. This meant, however, that she had much further to travel to work, which was a problem as her mobility was dependent on a wheelchair.

The lengths to which women will go to get and keep a job are sometimes extraordinary. Other parts of their life will be sacrificed in order to do the job well, as in Debra's case:

> I desperately wanted to keep my job. To me that was being normal, bringing in my share of the money. But I also had to bring in money, or we wouldn't have existed. It became obvious that I couldn't have a social night life and work. It was one or the other. I was so tired, I couldn't cope. That upset one or two of my friends, who used to say I was lazy. I never argued with them. I actually had to spend the odd Saturday or Sunday in bed sometimes, just to gain the energy to get to work on the Monday. In later years, it was fascinating talking to my husband. He had the same problem when he first started work.

The majority of women in this study had been or were in paid employment, enjoyed their work immensely, and felt satisfied and fulfilled by it. Despite this, in looking for work, none had had positive experience of the Disablement Resettlement Service and the Disablement Resettlement Officers (DROs) whose task it is to place people with disabilities into employment. One women found them to be 'hopeless'. Another felt they needed more training. Another had found the DRO to whom she had been allocated quite hostile and uninformative. One woman said she felt the whole idea of a Disablement Resettlement Service was discriminatory because it meant treating people with disabilities differently to the rest of the population. She felt that the employment services formed to assist the general population should be made more aware of the specific requirements of those people with disabilities looking for work. For Dipu, 'there was this tremendous lack of communication . . . and information'.

A study of DROs in 1979 found that their attitudes tended to resemble those of employers. While they were found to be conscientious with a good knowledge of the local labour market, they had less knowledge of techniques of rehabilitation, job redesign and measures of self-help. Their focus and allegiance, therefore, seemed to be with employers rather than with their clients. The researcher, an American, expressed considerable surprise at the extent to which officials paid more attention to the views of employers and trade unions as against the broad constituency of people with disabilities themselves (Stubbins, 1981). However, this assumes a degree of uniformity in the views of people with disabilities which does not necessarily exist. Reservations have been expressed about the DRO service by other independent researchers (Lonsdale and Walker, 1984) as well as by internal reviews of the service (Manpower Services Commission, 1982). One of the problems with Disablement Resettlement Officers is that they are not always selected and recruited for their awareness of disability issues, but rather to reflect a rung in the Employment Service career structure. They receive very little training overall. It might also be more appropriate if they were located more clearly out in the labour market, persuading employers to modify premises and job designs, as well as educating employers about ways of taking on more people with disabilities.

Employment gives women many types of satisfaction. Primarily, it provides company and the possibility of being with other people. It gives women confidence and increases their experience and skills. It provides challenges and, in Dipu's case, had overcome loneliness:

> Since I started working everything has changed. I no longer feel lonely. I've made friends of my own accord. People accept me for whatever I am. I don't have to convince them of anything. I have my own friends now. Otherwise, they were all my husband's friends.

Some women describe employment as helping them not to give up and to overcome the immense frustrations they sometimes feel. Debra said that her disability had been her salvation in that it had forced her into thinking about her life in a different way:

> I think if it hadn't been for polio, I might have drifted through school and into any kind of job. Mine was one of the old schools where the boy has the career. So I do think it opened up a whole range of opportunities that might not have been around for me.

The need for flexible hours

Women have different employment needs to men because they are usually bringing up children and running a home, whether living with a man or not. Their decision to take on paid work as well is usually the result of a complex interaction of factors relating to the need for money, the availability of child care, self-confidence and the actual ability to get work. These are influenced by the woman's socio-economic position, her race, her education, her history of training and employment – in other words, her life chances. For a woman with a disability, this takes on particular meaning. From very early on in her life, she may have had fewer opportunities in education, training and encouragement to plan and think in career terms than either disabled or non-disabled men and other women. She is also more likely than other women to encounter the assumption that she will not want a career or paid work, which in turn is based on the assumption of dependency on a husband.

Perry's (1984) study found a tendency for women with disabilities to feel they were less likely to attract a supportive spouse than men with disabilities: consequently they experienced greater pressure to take on the breadwinner role than other women. At the same time they felt limited by traditional attitudes to women and employment which was exacerbated by being disabled. Nearly three-quarters of the women interviewed wanted some form of paid work for the overriding reason that they needed money. Despite this, there was a high proportion of 'discouraged' workers in her sample who felt they stood little chance in the labour market because work was organised in a way that was inimical to their lives and requirements and because there was so much unemployment generally. All around them, women with disabilities see an expansion of training schemes for young people and adults and hear the official ideology that work is available for all who want it. At the same time, they are likely to experience the low expectations of their teachers and specialist career officers, telling them not to be unrealistic in relation to their own abilities (Bookis, 1983).

Women generally need flexible hours of work at certain stages of their life, such as when they are bringing up children. Women with disabilities have these same needs when they bring up their children, but like Jule, they sometimes also express a more general need for part-time work that is non-discriminatory and has 'full-time' status:

I like to do a challenging job, something I can get my brain around. I like to be well paid. I also like to feel I have some flexibility over working hours. This is a job share. It works very well. I work with my colleague, we both do two and a half days each week. Full-time work is quite tiring.

Jule also recognised that not all women with disabilities either need or want fewer working hours, and she felt that this should be an option available to all those people who wished to work more flexible hours for a variety of reasons. This creates a whole set of problems in relation to social security, although even if it didn't, the range of appropriate part-time jobs is simply not available. Those that do exist are usually in the service sector, such as cleaning and waitressing – physically tiring manual jobs which may be inappropriate for a woman with a physical disability.

The problem with somebody with my sort of condition is that I can't work full-time in a normal capacity. I certainly couldn't go out at nine and come back at five. It's the structure again. I can't earn. I either stay on disability benefit because I'm unfit for work, or I have to earn enough money, which I can't do on a part-time basis.

Two recently expanding types of employment which potentially could resolve this dilemma are now almost exclusively female, i.e. homeworking and part-time work. The reason women tend to occupy these jobs is because they make it easier to combine child care and housework with paid work. There is now growing evidence that women who are disabled and/or black are also doing these kinds of jobs as a response to discrimination against them in the labour market. However, both homework and part-time work are often low-paid and hazardous to health and family life (Bisset and Huws, 1984; Hurstfield, 1979). Homeworking presents additional problems for women with disabilities: it intensifies and compounds existing isolation; it increases invisibility; it often makes them feel undermined and undervalued; it is usually a second-best option to other employment; it has health and safety problems for women whose health already may be at risk; and it is poorly paid and exploitative (Ashok *et al.*, 1985; Bisset and Huws, 1984).

Likewise, part-time work presents its own hazards. Just as it is seen to be a solution for women with young children, so is it seen to be a solution for women whose disabilities make it difficult for them to work a full day or who wish to return to work gradually after a long absence. However, a study of 1,243 people with multiple sclerosis found that opportunities for part-time work for people with disabilities were very limited both for existing and new employees. While most employers would accept one or two hours' reduction in daily working time, 'anything in excess of this would lead the employer to start thinking in terms of early retirement with some sort of disability pension' (Davoud and Kettle, 1980, p. 60).

Although part-time work is expanding in most Western European countries, its growth in the UK has been very marked. While this should be an optimistic sign for women, it rarely is because so many part-time jobs are geared to the needs of industry to find more cost-effective ways of working rather than to the needs of women for more flexible hours of work (Lonsdale, 1987). Women with disabilities face an additional hurdle if they wish to do part-time work because of certain features in the structure of social security benefits.

There is no provision in Britain whereby people can combine part-time work with the receipt of partial benefits – in sharp contrast to many other European countries (Robbins, 1982). A person is judged as either capable or incapable of full-time work. Despite this, 4 per cent of people with disabilities are available for, and would like to, work, but are only able to undertake it part-time. Fifty-three per cent of employed women with disabilities are already working in part-time jobs. Over one-third of all employed women with disabilities felt that their disability affected the number of hours they could work, in contrast to just over one-quarter of employed men with disabilities (Martin *et al.*, 1989). However, as yet there is no provision for defining a reduced capacity for work which takes account of the complex and imprecise circumstances of individuals in order that they can receive a combination of reduced benefits with part-time wages. In very limited circumstances, someone can earn small amounts of money without forfeiting their benefits.

For instance, under certain circumstances someone who is disabled can earn up to a certain amount per week (£27.00 in 1989) before their entitlement to benefit is affected. These earnings are known as 'therapeutic' and the work done to obtain them must be considered to be for temporary, rehabilitative purposes only by a medical doctor. Working this way on a regular basis will invalidate the claim for benefit. This system forces many men and women with disabilities to become dependent on the state when they wish to work. It therefore also inhibits their integration into normal life, and embodies a view that people are either totally disabled or totally able-bodied. The reality, however, is that people are rarely 'fit' or 'unfit' but fall on a continuum of work capacity dependent sometimes on mental or physical factors such as having an impairment, and other times on social factors such as having to care for children, as well as the demands of the particular employment.

Even people who are not severely disabled tend to work fewer hours per week than other full-time employees, which is thought to be responsible for making their earnings significantly less than those of the general population (Martin and White, 1988, p. 17). Consequently, there is now a growing and urgent need for a 'partial capacity' social security benefit so that people can be more flexible in their working arrangements, combining part-time work and the receipt of social security (see Chapter 8). This would more accurately reflect the experience of disability in relation to paid work. A number of women in the present study expressed the need for greater flexibility in this respect. The ability to combine paid work and social security is already a practice adopted in the UK for retirement pensioners, who may earn a realistic wage before their pension begins to be reduced. The policy of accommodating reduced capacity rather than total incapacity for work is already adopted in at least seventy-nine countries around the world (Robbins, 1982). The introduction of such a policy is extremely important for people with degenerative illnesses such as muscular dystrophy, arthritis, Parkinson's disease, lupus, or multiple sclerosis, which is especially characterised by fatigue. Given that illnesses such as multiple sclerosis and arthritis predominantly affect women, they would benefit particularly from such a change. Just as importantly, it will contribute to a conceptual change which recognises the relative nature of disability.

Employment and unemployment

The feelings women have about their lack of opportunities are borne out by actual labour market experience. In their survey of disability, the OPCS found that only a minority of disabled adults were in paid work compared to the majority of the non-disabled population.

There was also much less difference between the proportions of men and women under pension age in paid work among the disabled population – 33 per cent of men compared with 29 per cent of women – than between men and women generally. Unlike the general population, however, unmarried women with disabilities were less likely to work than married women with disabilities. Generally, wives were less likely than husbands to be in paid work whichever was the disabled partner, except, surprisingly, in families where there were dependent children. As might be expected, severity of disability had a significant effect on the likelihood of an adult who was disabled being in paid work. While 48 per cent of people with the least severe disabilities were in paid work, only 2 per cent with the most severe disabilities were. The same pattern was shown for women, although a smaller proportion of women worked at all levels than men. The overall conclusion drawn by the survey was that disability clearly affected someone's chances of being in paid employment (Martin and White, 1988, pp. 12–14).

Women with disabilities face a double barrier to being in paid employment because when they do work, their earnings are likely to be concentrated at the lowest end of the earnings league. A number of studies have found evidence of a downward mobility and a drift into unemployment after the onset of disability (Buckle, 1971; Blaxter, 1976; Davoud and Kettle, 1980; Mitchell, 1981). The negative financial effect this has is exacerbated by an additional finding that only 22 per cent of disabled adults live in a family unit in which at least one person was earning. The large majority of families in which a member is disabled, therefore, are dependent on state benefits.

In comparing the average gross weekly earnings that people of working age receive from full-time employment, people who are disabled earn less than the working population in general. At the highest level women with disabilities working in non-manual jobs had earnings that were 94 per cent of the earnings of all women working in non-manual jobs. This contrasted with women working in manual jobs, where the earnings of women with disabilities were only 88 per cent of the earnings of all women in manual work (Martin and White, 1988, p. 17).

The explanations offered for this finding by the authors are the constraints on the type of work which people with disabilities are able to undertake, the fact that people who are disabled are on average older than the general population (even among non-pensioners) which may limit the kind of work they can do, and the fact that people in lower-paid occupations are more likely to become disabled. Another set of explanations, however, might equally well be found in the demands of the labour market itself. Employment tends not to be oriented towards the needs of potential employees, except when there are shortages of labour. Certain groups are disadvantaged for complex reasons related to the way in which our society and economy are organised, and this often finds expression in discrimination such as against women and minority groups (Lonsdale, 1985). As Chapter 6 shows, there is growing evidence that people who are disabled face discrimination when applying for jobs. A failure to implement policies facilitating the entry of disabled people into employment such as the quota scheme, described below, has also played a part.

Generally, unemployment is far higher for people with disabilities. According to the 1985 Labour Force Survey, the unemployment rate for all people of working age was 10.7 per cent, but for those whose health problems or disabilities limited the paid work they could do, the rate was more than double at 23.4 per cent. It is difficult to obtain accurate unemployment rates for women. Most official statistics underestimate them because the official definition of unemployment is different to the experience of most women (Martin and Roberts, 1984). Women tend not to go through official channels for registering as unemployed, finding work or getting retrained. Using a conventional definition of unemployment as being available for work and actively seeking work, however, the overall unemployment rates for economically active men and women with disabilities is still far higher than for others. In 1985 these were 27 per cent and 20 per cent respectively, compared to 11 per cent and 9 per cent of economically active men and women generally (Martin *et al.*, 1989). Using less restrictive criteria of unemployment than the official ones, Townsend (1979) estimated the unemployment rates for men and women of working age who are disabled to be even higher at 28 per cent and 56 per cent respectively.

Similar findings have been made in the United States in respect of the participation in paid work of women with disabilities, wage discrimination and unemployment rates. Kutner's (1984) study of 148 women and 184 men with disabilities also provides evidence to refute the view that women do not desire job retraining after the onset of disability. Although both men and women experienced discrimination by employers, this discrimination was directed at some women not only because of their disability, but also because of their alleged home and family responsibilities.

Very few women want to be financially dependent. A strategy which some women are adopting or hoping to adopt is that of running their own business. This, it is hoped, will give them the flexibility they require and the means of bringing in an independent income and supporting themselves. Those women who had created their own businesses seemed to be running them very successfully in terms of keeping going for long periods of time, although it was not always easy to bring in enough money to live on. Nadia's reasons for earning a living this way were clear:

> I didn't have to be at a certain place at nine and finish at five. I was my own boss. I could dictate what times I worked, and I could rest if I was flaked out. And write reports at twelve o'clock at night if I happened to be well at that time. So, from that point of view, it gave me the freedom to work.

As well as the independence and freedom of being self-employed, there were also pitfalls in the pressures of running their own business and the stresses and strains of not wanting one's clients to feel they are getting anything less than a perfect service. One woman would not tell her clients that she had multiple sclerosis, because, 'the last thing you want is for people to suspect that the one they trusted in the first place is no longer in control'. But this itself put her under tremendous pressure. Two other women ran cookery classes and shorthand and typing classes from home. Another woman spoke of her plans to open a restaurant with other family members. Interestingly, this was also partly a response to the racism she had encountered in the labour market and partly due to her desire to start up such a business.

A problem confronting women with disabilities who wish to do paid work has been the surplus of labour. While this seems to be changing due to an earlier decline in the birthrate which will lead to anticipated shortages of school-leavers in the 1990s, there are still hurdles for a woman with a disability trying to get a job. Women are still subject to a stereotype which lessens their chances or excludes them from certain types of employment. The ideology that women do and should give precedence to their homes and families over paid employment has determined the kinds of paid work they can do. Expectations about women's role are in turn upheld and reinforced by the nature of paid work as well as a great deal else in the social, political and economic fabric of society (Lonsdale, 1987). The stereotype relating to women's work has a powerful impact on women with disabilities because they are often also judged to be incapable of work, whether or not such capacity has ever been tested (Perry, 1984, p. 14). Despite this, many women must work. For Jule, who left school with no eligibility to social insurance benefits, working was a necessity.

> There's always the assumption that women with disabilities don't work...but I had no option but to find work. There were no other benefits for me.

For Debra, too, paid work was essential:

> I was one of the first who grew up in a one-parent family. My mother had a widow's war pension and had to work herself. So it was expected that I work. In fact she said she couldn't keep me, I'd have to have a job.

Labour market policy

Policy approaches to the employment of people with disabilities can be grouped as follows. First, they may focus on the characteristics of the person concerned and attempt to reduce the effect of disability by rehabilitation and training, or if that is judged impossible, by providing sheltered employment or employer subsidies to compensate for an assumed lower rate of productivity on the part of the worker with the disability. Alternatively, policies may focus on the workplace, either regulating employer behaviour or altering the nature of the environment and the tasks associated with the job, and providing appropriate transport facilities to and from work. The rationale for adopting a particular policy may be pragmatic, i.e. to meet shortages of labour or to reduce the costs of disability benefits; or it may be normative, i.e. to equalise access to jobs based on the view that everyone has the right to employment or the right to equal opportunities.

Most labour market policies consist of a combination of the two approaches and both rationales, although at different times, different ones may predominate. For instance, in Britain a quota scheme and some form of mobility and transport policy (based on private, not public transport) exist alongside rehabilitation and sheltered employment programmes. Similarly in the USA, employer subsidies and sheltered employment operate in the context of civil rights legislation which outlaws discrimination against people with disabilities. There is not the same emphasis on employer regulation through quota schemes as there is in many European countries. In the USA, anti-discrimination is stressed rather than the direct intervention in the labour market which quota schemes imply. The onus, therefore, is on the individual's alleging discrimination to prove it, rather than the onus being on employers to ensure they have a fair representation of people with disabilities in their workforce.

Focusing on the individual

Rehabilitation through some form of sheltered employment tends to play a prominent part in disability policy in most industrialised countries. In Britain, sheltered employment was originally conceived as a bridging experience to employment. More recently, however, sheltered workshops have tended to become permanent places of employment providing little therapy, rehabilitation or work satisfaction. They are intended for people whose productivity is estimated to be only one-third of that which might be expected. In a number of European countries, including those with generally progressive policies such as the Netherlands and Sweden, women form a minority of employees in sheltered workshops. In the present study, no woman had had experience of such employment.

Sheltered employment has often been heavily criticised for failing to provide a stimulating environment and for enforcing the segregation of many people with disabilities at work. As a means of overcoming these disadvantages, a new form of sheltered work has developed in Britain whereby about 5,000 people with severe disabilities are subsidised by the state to work in open employment. Known as Sheltered Placement Schemes, individuals in these jobs have their wages subsidised according to their lower productivity. Their employer assesses their output relative to an able-bodied employee and accordingly pays a proportion of their wage. The remainder is subsidised through a complex arrangement involving other 'sponsoring' employers from the state or charitable sectors.

The advantages of such schemes over sheltered employment are that they allow people with disabilities to work in ordinary employment settings which offer a greater variety of job opportunities. They are usually also more convenient geographically for employees. Certainly, their attraction must also lie in the fact that they are considerably cheaper than the large loss-making workshops. They have been criticised, however, as being a form of cheap labour, although the link to productivity was undoubtedly introduced with this in mind. Of greater importance, perhaps, is the basis on which assumptions of lower productivity are made, and the danger that such assumptions will remain static regardless of improvements in output. Additionally there may be difficulties related to differential systems and wages paid to certain workers. The scheme has been subject to an internal evaluation by the Department of Employment which was largely favourable. As with most of these kinds of reports, there is no data on women, but a substantial proportion of the jobs filled were predominantly in male occupations (Jones *et al.*, 1988).

A number of different types of subsidy operate. In Britain, a four-month job introduction subsidy was introduced in 1977 for employers who agreed to take on workers with disabilities. Similarly, in the USA a system of subsidising the wage costs of certain workers exists through tax credits. A New Jobs Tax Credit scheme came into effect in 1977, to encourage the hiring of certain groups. This was replaced by the Targeted Jobs Tax Credit, which provided a two-year subsidy to designated groups of workers including those with disabilities (Haveman *et al.*, 1984). There is some evidence that a high proportion of these subsidised workers do not retain employment for a substantial period of time. This is clearly a hazard of time-limited subsidies as against the more permanent subsidy of the Sheltered Placement Schemes. However, the former is not based on an assumption of lower productivity: rather it attempts to overcome the prejudice of employers against hiring certain groups of workers.

Focusing on the workplace

For some time, most organisations of and for people with disabilities have argued strongly and vehemently for better and more equal access to the labour market for individuals who are or become disabled. One of the keys to their integration into employment has sometimes been seen to be a policy of positive discrimination or quotas. Quotas operate in a number of European countries, with figures of 2 per cent in the Netherlands, 6 per cent in Germany, 10 per cent in the private sector and 3 per cent in the public sector in France, and 15 per cent in Italy, with different weightings applied to different categories of disability. In Britain, a system operates whereby employers with 20 or more employees have a statutory duty to employ a quota of 3 per cent of registered disabled people. Employers who are below their quota are not allowed to engage anyone who is not a registered disabled person without first obtaining a permit to do so. Infringing the law, in theory, can lead to a maximum of three months' imprisonment and a maximum fine of £400 for an individual employer, and £2,000 for a corporate body. This rarely occurs in practice, and has never occurred as far as imprisonment is concerned. In most countries, it is unusual for quotas to be enforced strongly, with the possible exception of the Federal Republic of Germany, which levies an automatic fine on employers who do not fulfil their quota obligations.

In Britain, whenever the quota system has not been enforced and has been threatened with abolition or with being weakened, there have been powerful reactions from many quarters demanding its retention and strengthening as a fundamental right of people with disabilities. People with disabilities and their organisations appear not to want to lose the quota system regardless of its alleged faults and unviability. Quotas have often been seen as especially relevant in periods of high unemployment, which have a tendency disproportionately to affect people with disabilities, whose unemployment rates, as has been shown, are far in excess not only of the general population but of other minority groups as well. Given the difficulties women face in the labour market, it could be argued that they stand to gain particularly by such a policy, assuming proper enforcement and a dedication and commitment to the principles behind the quota system by those charged with administering it.

The quota system in Britain has been largely unchanged since 1944, when it was first introduced. Its retention in some respects has been a hollow victory for people with disabilities because is has never been properly enforced by the agencies of central government, but has been left to fall into disrepute (except for one or two notable attempts by individual local authorities to use it in the spirit for which it was intended). Most government policy seems to have been tacitly to acknowledge the political unacceptability of abolishing quotas, leaving the system to languish as a policy which if not actually unworkable, is not being allowed to work.

The unpopularity of the quota scheme on the part of its administrators is puzzling. Of the total budget spent on employment assistance to people with disabilities in 1985–6, the vast majority (70 per cent) was spent on sheltered employment. A further 28 per cent was spent on Employment Rehabilitation Centres and Job Centre services. The remaining £1–2 million which is spent on administering the quota scheme is paltry by comparison (and may go some way to explaining why it has not been abolished despite strong motivations to do so on the part of a government ideologically committed to deregulation). The popularity of the quota scheme on the part of people with disabilities is less puzzling. Although it is almost universally acknowledged to be not working, it nonetheless represents the embodiment of a potentially powerful instrument of policy which not only outlaws discrimination but positively promotes the integration of people with disabilities into the labour force. It represents a strong form of positive discrimination which is intended to counteract the severe disadvantage which disability brings, to overcome the negative discrimination which people with disabilities face when looking for jobs either through prejudice or ignorance on the part of employers and the public generally, and to redress the extremely high rates of unemployment which this particular minority group experiences. Its operation and monitoring, however, need consistency and strong implementation if it is to be an effective instrument of policy.

In contrast to a policy of positive discrimination or quotas, is a policy of *encouraging* employers, rather than forcing them, to take on workers with disabilities. Employment subsidies do this through financial incentives, but a range of other measures is emerging which have no more of an inducement than a moral imperative. A 'Fit for

Work' award to employers who made 'outstanding achievements in the employment of disabled people' was introduced in 1979 as part of a wider attempt to deregulate the British labour market. A similar policy of attempting to encourage rather than insist on employers taking on employees with disabilities, called Positive Policies, had been tried earlier. Both had little effect on improving the employment opportunities of people with disabilities, and were more effective as a public relations exercise. A voluntary *Code of Good Practice on the Employment of Disabled People* was published in October 1984. This appears to have been the compromise reached by a government who could not abolish the quota system in the face of popular support, but who wanted to deregulate the labour market. The code is a source of information on financial and other assistance available for the employment of people with disabilities. It is a guide to good employment practice and the law, although it is non-statutory itself.

A statutory disclosure of company policy was introduced in regulations relating to the Companies Act in 1980. Since then, the annual reports of companies employing more than 250 people must contain a statement of the company's policy towards employing people with disabilities, covering recruitment, training and career development. Again, this has proved useful as a public relations exercise for companies, although there is no evidence that it has done anything to ensure that companies fulfil what still remains a legal responsibility to employ a certain proportion of people with disabilities. The great majority of companies still do not do so.

The focus and concentration of policy on the quota scheme, as well as campaigns attempting to influence policy, may have obscured the significance of other areas of concern and other potential policies. One of these is the possibility of anti-discrimination legislation or legislation along the lines of the United States civil rights legislation, updated to include people with disabilities in 1988. However, unlike the USA, there is no anti-discrimination legislation for people with disabilities in Britain. Such legislation might cover a wide range of areas such as education, housing, public transport, and physical access to public places, among others. Since all these things are related to employment, in that they affect an individual's ability to obtain work and to get to work, such legislation could facilitate employment, especially if it applied to both the private and public sectors. Anti-discrimination legislation running alongside a quota scheme might also offer a means of appeal on the part of people with disabilities themselves, although it is difficult to see how this could operate concurrently with the present provisions of the 1944 Disabled Persons (Employment) Act.

Another potential scheme is job-sharing. A number of job-share posts have emerged recently in some local authorities as part of their equal opportunities policies. Job-shares are often sought by women for a variety of reasons (Coyle and Skinner, 1988, p. 22). The conventional arrangement of employment, i.e. full-time work every day over a lifetime, is not convenient for people who would like both to work and be involved in their family, nor is it convenient for people who need more diverse and flexible working time, such as someone with a disability might. Women with disabilities who seek to work part of the time and yet also want the responsibility and commitment of interesting jobs which usually need to be done on a full-time basis, could benefit from a shared post. In the present study, only one woman, Jule, had worked in a job-share. She had found this very much suited her circumstances:

> It works very well. I work well with my colleague and we both do two and a half days each week. Full-time working is quite tiring...I think flexibility with the job-share has been the principle...I think it's important for women, and particularly people with disabilities. You can manage working a certain number of hours.

The considerable growth of part-time jobs in recent years reflects a continuing and, what appears to be, long-term change in the composition of the labour force in most industrialised countries. Consisting almost entirely of female employment, part-time jobs have however, been a response to demands for increased efficiency, greater productivity and profitability rather than to the needs of women or some people with disabilities. By contrast, job-share posts are an initiative designed to do the latter, to provide part-time work without its usual concomitant features of low pay, low levels of skill, and poor working conditions.

Equal opportunities legislation or the establishment of the principle that all people have an equal opportunity to employment is very different to the principle that people have a *right* to employment. The latter usually recognises the existence of disadvantage and tried to rectify it for particular groups. Simply outlawing discrimination does not necessarily ensure that people will be treated fairly or that they will always be able to claim redress under the law. There is a great deal of evidence of this from the Race Relations Act, the Sex Discrimination Act and the Equal Pay Act. By the same token, as we have seen with the quota scheme, having an entitlement or a guarantee of employment does not always provide it. It is probably necessary to enshrine in law both types of policy in order that individuals have redress against unfair or discriminatory practices while at the same time recognising that certain groups in our society are disadvantaged minorities.

Promoting good employment practices can take many forms, ranging from voluntary codes of good practice (such as those published by the Department of Employment for employers and the Trades Union Congress for trade unionists) to local authorities' awarding financial contracts only to those companies fulfilling certain requirements (such as the system of contract compliance operated by the Greater London Council until its demise, and some of the rules governing the award of federal grants in the USA).

Codes of practice which are neither statutory nor attach a financial incentive or penalty are likely to have less influence over the employment practices of companies than those which do. For instance, the voluntary code of practice operating in Britain lacks teeth. While there is much that is sound and admirable in the practices it advocates, there is no reason whatsoever why any employer should take any notice of it. By contrast, using the purchasing power of local or central government departments to induce better employment practices on the part of employers is potentially more effective in that it links the awarding of contracts to firms that comply with certain rules.

The Greater London Council was the first local authority in the United Kingdom to initiate contracts compliance in 1983, in an attempt to use its economic power to promote training at work, health and safety, pay and conditions, trade union rights and equal opportunities policies for minority groups. It did this by using certain sections of the Local Government Act 1972, which allowed local authorities to include certain requirements in standing orders for tenders and contracts. It attempted judiciously to balance the need for acting in a businesslike and competitive manner as required under the Competition Act 1980 (enabling sufficient companies to compete for tenders to ensure a favourable contract price) with regulating the practices of companies to whom contracts were awarded – for instance to comply with Acts such as the Race Relations Act 1976. Companies wishing to remain on an approved list of suppliers and contractors had to show that they were complying with the Council's equal opportunity requirements, although this was largely confined to women and ethnic minorities, as no comparable anti-discrimination legislation exists for people with disabilities.

From 1983, such a policy has been in direct opposition to central government's attempts to promote greater competitiveness, more privatisation and the deregulation of businesses from any constraints on their operations in the market place. Consequently, legislation was enacted to outlaw such practices, except in certain situations when it contradicted other legislation such as the Race Relations Act. Local authorities were to be able to query potential contractors on racial equality, but only in a specific way as laid down by law and only before a contract had been finalised.

The present situation, therefore, is one where mild and largely ineffective policies of promoting good employment practices for workers with disabilities exist, while more vigorous policies have been made illegal (e.g. contract compliance), or are not enforced (e.g. the quota scheme). It is likely however, that any serious commitment to improving the employment opportunities of people with disabilities will have to recognise that some degree of market regulation is necessary and that companies will need stronger incentives, if not enforceable quotas, to incorporate equal opportunities policies into their business practices.

8

The financial consequences of disability

The association between poverty and disability generally has been well documented, as has the failure of most distributive systems to provide for social needs. The relatively worse financial position of people with disabilities has persisted over time. As far back as 1969, the OPCS survey of disability in Britain found that, as a whole, the incomes of people with disabilities were lower than those for the general population, and that 39 per cent were living at or below the state poverty line (Harris *et al.*, 1972). Townsend's survey, undertaken at the same time, substantiated this, finding that people with disabilities generally had both lower incomes and fewer assets than people who were not disabled. In addition to this, he also found an association between poverty and degree of disability. With increasing incapacity, proportionately more people lived in households with incomes on or only marginally above the state poverty line. More than half of those with severe or appreciable incapacity were living in poverty or on the margins of poverty, compared to under a quarter of those with no incapacity. If the annuity values of the assets they owned were added to their net disposable income for the previous year and the resulting income expressed as a percentage of the state's poverty line, then still half of all people with a disability had an income on or below it, as against only 17 per cent of the non-disabled (Townsend, 1979, pp. 712–13).

Townsend's survey does not provide detailed information about the difference between the incomes of men and women with disabilities, although more women than men had gross earnings of less than two-thirds of average earnings. It also gives two telling examples of the poverty which women on their own can experience when disabled, and discusses the particular position of the housewife who is disabled, which will be discussed in more detail below. Various analyses of the income of women with disabilities have been done in the United States, and these have found that the impact of disability on women or female heads of household is particularly severe. Households headed by non-married women who are disabled have been found on average to be the poorest of all households (Mudrick, 1983a). Women with disabilities have also been found to earn considerably less than men with disabilities (Greenblum, 1977). In general, women with disabilities have been found to be at a greater economic disadvantage than men (Franklin, 1977).

In Britain, fewer studies have focused on the incomes of disabled women. However, a study of the financial consequences of illness and injury for over 2,000 people in 1976 found that, on average, they reported incomes significantly lower than the UK national estimate. Nearly one-quarter had an income below the poverty line. Average incomes were found to be lower, the greater the severity of the disability (Brittan, 1982). The Royal Commission on the Distribution of Income and Wealth found that the incomes of over half of all households headed by a person who was disabled were less than 120 per cent of the state poverty line. Again, poverty was found to increase in proportion to the severity of disability, (Layard *et al.*, 1978, p. 113). An analysis of the elderly in the 1980 General Household Survey found that 42 per cent of the non-disabled lived below the poverty line compared to 71 per cent of those who were severely disabled. Not only did disability exacerbate poverty among the elderly, but the incidence of poverty was significantly higher among women (Victor and Vetter, 1986). In 1983 this pattern was found still to persist, with 33 per cent of all people with disabilities living on or below the state poverty line compared with only 15 per cent of the rest of the population (Disability Alliance, 1987, p. 19).

The 1988 OPCS large-scale survey of the financial circumstances of almost six million people with disabilities living in private households in Britain has reinforced these findings. It has not only found evidence of greater poverty in disabled households than non-disabled households, but also that within the population who are disabled, some are poorer than others (Martin and White, 1988, p. 54). The survey collected information about two types of income:

usual net disposable income, referring to normal income after income tax, national insurance contributions and housing costs had been deducted, and *net disposable resources*, referring to net disposable income minus additional regular expenditure due to disability. Equivalence scales were used to standardise incomes in order to take account of differences in family composition. These were the same scales used in the Family Expenditure Survey, enabling the survey data to be compared with data for the general population.

Consequently, a number of studies have now concluded that people with disabilities have a greater likelihood of falling into poverty during their lives. This is due to two main factors. First, someone with a disability is less likely to be in paid employment, less likely to have full-time work, and, therefore, more likely to have a lower income. Second, people incur additional costs through having a disability, not least of all due to requirements for practical assistance and personal care.

Lower incomes

The 1988 OPCS survey found that the average equivalent income of adults of working age who were disabled was 72 per cent of the average equivalent income of the general population of working age. A much smaller proportion of the adult population of working age who were disabled had incomes that were more than the average – 19 per cent compared with 42 per cent of the general population. The main reason for these differences was that adults of working age who were disabled were less likely to be earning a wage or salary than their non-disabled counterparts. Even among those disabled adults who were married, few had a partner who was in paid work. Consequently, their reliance on social security benefits was very high. Those people who depended on benefits had significantly lower incomes than those who had access to earned income. As discussed in the last chapter, fewer women than men were in paid employment, particularly if they were married. Of those disabled adults of working age who were married, 37 per cent of women and 49 per cent of men were in paid employment. This is much lower than is found in the general population, where 58 per cent of married women and 78 per cent of men are in paid work, although the male/female difference is roughly the same.

This pattern persists regardless of which one of the married couple is disabled. The wives of men who are disabled are less likely to be in paid employment than the husbands of women who are disabled. Similarly, when husbands themselves are disabled they are more likely to be in employment than when wives are disabled. The presence of dependent children did not seem to deter women from working. In addition to differences in participation in paid work between men and women, severity of disability also has a significant effect on the likelihood of someone being in paid work when age, sex and marital status are taken into account (Martin and White, 1988, pp. 12–14).

When considering people's net disposable resources, or their net disposable income minus what they have to spend on additional items related to their disability, their situation worsens. On average, 8 per cent of the income of a person who has a disability goes on disability-related expenditure. These additional expenses make people with disabilities worse off than the rest of the population, even though they are less likely to be in paid work and, therefore, to face work-related expenses. The average net disposable resources of disabled people of working age (again standardised by equivalence scales to take account of different family types) is 67 per cent of the income of the general population.

Additional living expenses

In addition to the findings concerning the lower incomes of people who are disabled, there have been a number of important studies on the specific additional costs that disability incurs. The findings of these studies differ, however, in their estimates of the additional costs of disability. Baldwin's (1976, 1977) work on the experience of families in which there are disabled children, identified extra costs in clothing, housekeeping, laundry, transport, heating, wear and tear on furniture, and the need for specific equipment such as housing adaptations. A later (1985) study, in which she compared the costs and incomes of families with a disabled child to those families without, found evidence of both additional costs and lower incomes when disability was present in the family. The lower incomes were caused by differences in the employment patterns of both parents, but this was particularly marked in the case of the mother. At the other end of the age spectrum, Nissel and Bonnerjea's (1982) study of the care of elderly people with disabilities came to very similar conclusions.

Further studies have found similar evidence of poverty and the incurring of extra costs among adults who are deaf, who use wheelchairs, who have both intellectual and physical disabilities, or who have a range of physical disabilities. All come to the same conclusion that all forms of disability have financial consequences for the individuals and families affected by them (Loach, 1976; Hyman, 1977; Buckle, 1983; Durward, 1981). In addition to this information from small qualitative studies, there is also evidence on the additional costs which disability incurs from the large-scale survey data of the OPCS study. The study distinguished three types of expenditure: lump-sum purchases on items required solely as a consequence of disability; regular expenditures also solely due to the disability; and additional expenses which people with disabilities incur on 'normal' items of expenditure (Martin and White, 1988, p. 36).

With regard to lump-sum purchases, 68 per cent of people in the survey had purchased at least one of a number of items required specifically for disability, such as special furniture, a wheelchair, or vehicle adaptations. Of the 16 per cent of people who had made these purchases during the previous year, the average amount spent was £78.00 (almost half of average weekly earning at the time of the survey), although there was considerable variation between individuals. The more severely disabled someone was, the more they were likely to have spent. People who were most severely disabled had spent on average £157.00, while those who were least disabled had spent £56.00 on average.

With regard to regular expenditure on items directly related to the disability such as chemists items, prescriptions and visits to the hospital or clinic, most people also incurred additional costs. Apart from chemist items, 60 per cent of people had incurred extra expenditure, estimated to average £2.20 per week. Again, there was considerable individual variation. There was also a marked increase in such expenditure with increasing severity of the disability, with the most severely disabled spending twice as much on average per week.

Often people who are disabled need to spend more money on things that are an everyday requirement for everyone. For instance, their travel costs may be greater due to the inaccessibility of much public transport. They may require additional heating, have extra laundry costs, face greater wear and tear on carpets or clothes, and have particular need of a telephone. The most common item of this kind of expenditure was found by the survey to be extra fuel costs for heating or hot water. Almost three-quarters of the sample spent on average £6.70 per week on this, but this increased to £8.50 for those people who were most severely disabled.

Excluding lump-sum purchases because of the difficulties in calculating these accurately, the survey's authors calculated that adults of working age who are disabled spend on average £6.70 per week on the needs that arise out of having a disability. This increased to £13.10 for people who were the most severely disabled. Expenditure on such items, however, was found to be constrained by income. Virtually one-quarter of the sample needed to spend more than they did to accommodate their disability, but could not afford to do so. This was mainly found to be a problem experienced by poorer people.

The OPCS survey's small estimates of the additional costs relating to disability are in stark contrast to the earlier studies referred to. Hyman's (1977) study, undertaken almost ten years prior to the OPCS survey, found that wheelchair users incurred additional costs averaging £14.13 per week. Buckle's (1983) study of 128 households living with mental handicap found that additional expenditure averaging £19.50 per week was incurred. Both studies therefore found evidence of average additional expenditure which was some two to three times greater than that found by the OPCS surveys, even before the real value of these amounts at the time of the OPCS survey had been taken into account.

The first possible reason for these discrepancies might lie in the lower threshold of disability used by the 1988 OPCS survey. As outlined in Chapter 2, this survey used a wider definition of disability than that used in the 1971 OPCS survey (Harris, 1971). Consequently, it estimated the adult population of people with disabilities to be just under six million, twice the estimate of three million reached by the earlier study. The effect of including less severely disabled people in the survey count might be expected to lower the average additional costs of disability. However, unlike the earlier survey, it did not restrict its definition of disability to physical disablement, nor did it exclude people living in institutions. The effect of this might be expected to produce higher estimates of the prevalence of disability.

Another more likely reason for the low estimate of additional expenditure can be found in the methodology used. A survey is a blunt instrument with which to measure certain things. The OPCS report states: 'in general, it has been found that small-scale studies using semi-structured interviews, often carried out by the researchers, find higher proportions than large-scale studies using structured interviews carried out by professional interviewers,' (Martin and White, 1988, p. 35). This general methodological problem includes the shorter amount of time devoted to obtaining information. For instance, finding out about financial costs was only one of a number of items of information being sought. In response to this problem, the Disablement Income Group undertook a more lengthy, qualitative study of the costs of disability for a group of thirteen people with severe physical disabilities. All were in receipt of at least one of the two main disability-related benefits, Attendance Allowance and Mobility Allowance. All would have been included in the most severely disabled category for the OPCS survey. The DIG study focused on the same items of expenditure used in the OPCS survey. Two questionnaires were administered, one consisting of the OPCS questions and taking twenty minutes to answer, the other consisting of questions considered more appropriate by DIG and taking an hour to answer.

The findings on extra costs differed substantially from the OPCS survey. The average weekly extra costs were found to be considerably greater than those in the OPCS survey, even when using the OPCS's own questions. On average, the additional weekly costs were found to be £41.84 using the OPCS questions, and £65.94 using the DIG questions (Thompson *et al.*, 1988, p. 14). These amounts were 440 per cent and 694 per cent higher respectively than the OPCS survey's average estimates for the most severely disabled category of people in their sample. These dramatic differences were considered to be due to the greater responsiveness of the respondents to the DIG style of interviewing. The people interviewed were helped to think through what were very complex financial calculations. The fundamental problem with the OPCS survey in this area was felt to lie in its failure to go into sufficient detail or to probe deeply enough into the costs of disability.

Perhaps more important, though, is the third factor influencing how much extra is spent as a result of disability. The more integrated people with disabilities are in normal social and economic life, the more they will incur additional costs. For example, if a woman who is deaf wishes to attend a public meeting or lecture, she can only do so meaningfully if someone has been employed to sign for her or if she has the help of expensive equipment. With advances in technology, her potential and opportunity for leading a fully integrated life in a speaking world will increase considerably, but at extra cost. In estimating the additional costs of disability, therefore, it is not sufficient to rely only on what people spend and the actual costs they incur, but what costs would be incurred in order to lead an integrated life.

The additional costs of trying to lead integrated and sociable lives were certainly felt by most women in the present study, virtually all of whom had felt financial hardship. None had extravagant lifestyles, but all experienced additional costs of being disabled that went far beyond the conservative average estimates of the OPCS survey. As well as the difficulties of finding decently paid jobs, there were the problems of the wear and tear on carpets of wheelchairs, the high cost of transport, the costs of special clothing, the costs of holidays if they were ever taken – which was rare – the enormous costs of good wheelchairs, and other items. Many women expressed a constant preoccupation with money, one saying she felt she was forever 'scrimping and saving'.

One of the hazards of independent living is that people have all the costs of general upkeep to bear without necessarily having the income to do it. The costs include the usual wear and tear on housing as well as specific kinds of wear and tear related to the disability, as Anita explained:

I don't need very much by way of material things but, you see, one of the things which is coming up which is going to be quite costly, is that I've got to have all the window frames done. So that means I've got to have all the cracks done and they've got to be repainted and redone. That will probably be in the region of two or three hundred pounds. And it's trying to just portion it out so that it doesn't all come together. I mean, I've just had the carpets cleaned – it's the wheelchair, it makes the carpets filthy. It's this central wheel. It's been like a road running through here. And if you drop something, you can't clean it up. But you have to have the whole place carpeted because of falling over. Not many people have to recarpet.

Despite the obvious extra hardships someone with a disability has to face, there are still assumptions made that they can afford certain things. Felicity felt that her voluntary help from a charitable organisation had stopped because they thought she could afford to pay for it. In fact, she was having to take in boarders to make ends meet and to be able to stay in her own home after she had been widowed. She also felt that the voluntary organisation which was helping her begrudged doing so because she had a daughter who they felt could help instead:

> My daughter used to come home from work for lunch, and if she sat down to her lunch, I felt really guilty if the other ladies were here doing things. And there was a terrible atmosphere.

Social security

The majority of adults who are disabled live in family units where there are no earners and their reliance on state benefits as their main source of income is high. Fifty-eight per cent of the income of the families of people who are disabled comes from state benefits, compared to only 24 per cent from earnings and 18 per cent from other sources such as savings or redundancy payments (Martin and White, 1988, pp. 19, 26).

The system of state support for people with disabilities in Britain is extremely fragmented. The first form of general but limited financial provision from the state became available through the Poor Law. However, more specific provision came later with payments for industrial injury and war disablement emerging in the nineteenth and early twentieth centuries. During the first part of this century, general provision came from national health insurance benefits for people who were employed and public assistance for the poor. Aside from this, people had to rely on charitable support and friendly society benefits. With the introduction of the Beveridge scheme in the 1940s, essentially the same pattern of state benefits prevailed – war pensions, industrial injuries, national insurance sickness benefit, and national assistance.

The present system of state benefits to assist with the costs of disability can only really be said to have been in existence in its present form since 1971. In that year, an Invalidity Pension was introduced, replacing long-term sickness benefit, as an alternative to earnings for those people whose disability made it impossible for them to take paid employment. An Attendance Allowance was introduced at the same time for severely disabled people who needed a lot of care. In a sense this recognised that financial support was necessary for two different reasons: to replace earnings and to cover certain additional costs which disability incurs. In 1976, a further additional cost was recognised when the Mobility Allowance was introduced for people who were severely restricted in walking. Both allowances are extremely small sums of money, quite inadequate to the cover the actual costs of attendant care or mobility requirements. In 1989, the weekly Mobility Allowance amounted to only 10 per cent of average earnings, while even the higher rate of Attendance Allowance was only 14 per cent of average weekly earnings.

The Invalidity Pension has always had a serious drawback. As a National Insurance-based benefit, it can only be claimed by people who have contributed sufficiently to the National Insurance Fund. By definition, this means they have to have been in employment and to have earned over a certain amount. Therefore, certain groups are excluded from it, namely those who become disabled before starting work or who have been out of the labour market for some time, such as women caring for children.

To meet the needs of the first group, a Non-Contributory Invalidity Pension (NCIP) was introduced in 1975. It was set at 60 per cent of the level of ordinary Invalidity Pension, establishing a principle that employed people were more deserving of financial support if they became too disabled to work because they had *earned* it. Married or cohabiting women were excluded from claiming NCIP. In response to the outcry over their exclusion, a benefit called Housewives' Non-Contributory Invalidity Pension (HNCIP) was introduced for them in 1977. This proved to be a back-handed gain. In addition to proving incapacity for paid employment, married women had to undergo a 'household duties test' to prove their incapacity for unpaid work in the home. Apart from often being a degrading and humiliating test, the benefit implied that domestic labour was the duty of women.

In the face of mounting criticism and sustained campaigning against the benefit, the question of the household duties test was referred to the National Insurance Advisory Committee in 1978 after only one year of its being in operation. Despite the Committee's recommendation two years on that the test be phased out, the question was again referred to an internal civil service review. Three years later, this review also recommended abolishing the test. At the same time as these lengthy reviews were in progress, an EEC directive was issued giving its member states until December 1984 to ensure that men and women were treated equally in social security matters (European Community, 1978). Consequently, at the eleventh hour the Health and Social Security Act 1984 was altered to provide for the abolition of NCIP and HNCIP. Both were replaced by a new benefit, the Severe Disablement Allowance, which despite its appearance of being gender neutral, was still to be paid at the lower level of 60 per cent of Invalidity Pension and was still predominantly paid to women.

A benefit for people who have given up paid work to care for someone who is disabled, the Invalid Care Allowance (ICA) also originally excluded married or cohabiting women. This benefit was not deemed to fall within the scope of the EEC Directive until March 1985, when the Social Security Appeal Tribunal ruled that it was illegal. This led to claims for the benefit from approximately 125,000 married women who had previously been ineligible to claim it.

Women have always come out badly in the provision of financial benefits, both generally and in relation to disability. The National Council of Women's evidence to the Beveridge Committee drew attention to this, as have subsequent women's groups and organisations (Brown, 1984). Despite this, little has changed over the years, as the story of Invalidity Benefits shows. Women's position in the labour market has also put them at a disadvantage in a social security system which is determined by particular patterns of work, both in the United Kingdom and the USA (Lonsdale, 1985; Alcock, 1987; Kutza, 1981).

The social security system in Britain is organised in such a way that it severely disadvantages female claimants, particularly when they are disabled. Disability benefits do not usually distinguish between different kinds of disabilities, but their rules of eligibility make the cause and onset of disability important in determining who gets what benefit. State benefits are based on a patriarchal conception of work in that they are usually linked to employment histories in the market place. Unpaid labour in the home does not usually count towards disability benefits. Consequently, most men tend to receive benefits that are legitimated by being linked to national insurance contributions or by being justifiable compensation from the community for work- or war-related injuries. Most women tend to receive benefits that are stigmatised welfare payments. This is true of both the United States and Britain. In the USA, few women have disability benefits in their own right, which also appears to be due to the type and extent of their participation in the labour force. Both Disability Insurance and Workman's Compensation benefits are contingent upon labour market participation, and Supplemental Security Income is based on incapacity for paid work in the labour market (Kutza, 1981; Mudrick, 1983a). There is also evidence of differential and unequal treatment of men and women in other social security systems, such as the Dutch disability insurance legislation. In the Netherlands women are more likely to lose their disability benefits sooner than men because of the dominant views held by civil servants and the society at large about the labour market participation of women (Hermans, 1988).

Women are disadvantaged not only while they are of working age, but also when they grow old. A woman who has been disabled for much or most of her life will have had fewer opportunities to build up an adequate retirement income. In the present study, many women were concerned about the future and how they would be living and how they would manage financially as they went into old age.

There is no coherent philosophy behind the system of disability benefits in Britain. Benefits are based on a number of different principles such as the cause of the disability, whether fault can be attributed, and whether contributions or premiums have been paid (Brown, 1984). As a result, the system has led to the growth of a number of groups who have different vested interests in maintaining it in its inefficient and unduly complex form. For instance, war pensioners resist any moves to undermine their special status, and the trade union movement lobbies to protect the industrial injuries scheme for its members. Both these interest groups favour men. The needs and interests of women with disabilities have been consistently neglected.

In periods of high unemployment, social security becomes crucially important as a resource system for many people. Large numbers of women with disabilities rely on state cash benefits. In 1987, 214,000 women received Invalidity Benefit. A further 158,000 women received Severe Disablement Allowance (SDA), and an unknown number relied on Supplementary Benefits – now called Income Support (DSS Social Security Statistics, 1988). Over three-quarters of the women in Perry's (1984) study were dependent on state benefits, and nearly half her sample's only source of income was state benefits. Less than one in ten of the women she interviewed were entitled to contributory national insurance benefits, i.e. benefits as of right. The remainder had to undergo various tests to prove their entitlement to financial support.

In addition to the benefits being inadequate, there are other disincentives for women who are disabled to claim them. A number of social security offices are inaccessible, and claiming benefits can be a frustrating business, as one woman in the present study found:

> When I went to sign on, I couldn't get in, the door was too small. So I had to phone up. They said if I came down they would bring my papers outside and I could sign on outside. I thought, this can't be for real. No one else has their personal business discussed outside an office building. So I said no. Then for about two or three weeks they were going to two or three different departments to find out what happens when a disabled person cannot get in. Eventually I signed on by post. And little things like they don't even send you a stamped addressed envelope, so you have to pay to sign on. When you're on a tight budget, every penny counts.

The main disability benefit in Britain is Invalidity Benefit. Paid at the same rate as retirement pension, it is dependent on the individual having paid sufficient national insurance contributions. In 1987, just under one million people received it, of whom the majority were men despite the higher incidence of disability among women (DSS Social Security Statistics, 1988). This is not surprising however, given the employment histories of women, their lower participation in the labour market and their lower rates of pay – all of which make it more difficult for a woman to have fulfilled the contributory conditions for national insurance benefits.

Women who are not eligible for Invalidity Benefit can try claiming Severe Disablement Benefit. This is a second-rate alternative because it is set at only 60 per cent of the level of Invalidity Benefit. It is available for people who have become disabled before their twentieth birthday or who are assessed as being at least 80 per cent disabled. In 1987 just over a quarter of a million people received it, of whom the majority were women (see Table 8.1). There is some evidence that the disadvantages married women faced under the old HNCIP scheme are pursuing them into the new SDA scheme. Over 71 per cent of male or single female beneficiaries of SDA have been 'passported' on to it because they were previously recipients of NCIP. However, only 6.5 per cent of married women receive SDA on this basis. The majority have to be tested to ensure they are 80 per cent disabled, and married women tend to be less successful in their claim (Disability Alliance, 1988, pp 27–8). Another particularly worrying element of SDA is the stringent residency requirement that goes with it. A claimant must have lived in Britain for ten out of twenty years. This rule will disproportionately exclude more black people from claiming it, in so far as they may be immigrants to Britain.

Table 8.1   *Men and women on Invalidity Benefit and Severe Disablement Benefit, 1987*

	Invalidity Benefit	*Severe Disablement Benefit*
Proportion of women	22%	61%
Proportion of men	78%	39%
Total number	968,000	260,000

Source: Department of Social Security Statistics, 1988.

A higher proportion of appeals to social security appeals tribunals against Invalidity Benefit decisions are successful than appeals against SDA decisions. This again makes Invalidity Benefit a more advantageous benefit for claimants (DSS Social Security Statistics, 1988). Women who are not eligible for either Invalidity Pension or SDA can claim a means-tested benefit, Income Support (previously named Supplementary Benefit) if their income is below the state poverty level. In 1987, 350,000 people under retirement age received this on the grounds of being sick or disabled, a 75 per cent increase in recipients since 1979 (Social Security Advisory Committee, 1988, p. 33). Until 1984, married or cohabiting women in such a situation could not claim this in their own right if their husbands or partners were employed. Although the rules were changed under pressure from the EEC, many married or cohabiting women are still effectively excluded, as the new rules set requirements which women often cannot fulfil despite the fact that they are often more likely to be claimants. Income Support is also used to supplement other benefits if their levels are below the poverty level. Eight per cent of Invalidity Benefit recipients claim Income Support, compared with 52 per cent of SDA recipients, making more women likely to be dependent on this means-tested part of the social security system despite the difficulties married women experience claiming it (SSAC, 1988, p. 21).

The disability benefits that are paid to people who become disabled at work or during war service are more generous than any of those already mentioned. The Industrial Disablement Benefit and the War Disablement Pension rates are considerably higher than the rates of all other disability benefits. Their basic rate is 163 per cent the rate of Invalidity Benefit and 271 per cent the rate of SDA. Both the industrial and war benefit usually have a number of additional allowances on top of their basic rate, which mean that these claimants theoretically, and often in practice, can receive nearly four times more per week than other claimants. In 1985, 186,000 people received Industrial Disablement Benefit and 220,000 received a War Disablement Pension. A breakdown of recipients according to sex is not available, although most are likely to be men, given the nature of industrial work and war service.

Thus there is a variety of weekly disability pensions with a wide range of rates. The way in which the benefit system is structured ensures that the majority of women receive the lowest rate and the majority of men the highest rates. Even the amounts paid to adult dependants vary, with SDA recipients getting less than others. For example, a married man disabled during the Falklands War with a wife and two children to support, could get a War Pension which (with supplements for unemployability, age clothing and loss of mobility) would be five times the amount a woman with the same disability and an unemployed husband and two children could get were she eligible for SDA.

The disability benefits system therefore not only makes spurious distinctions between people with disabilities that have arisen in different circumstances, but is gender-biased to the detriment of women with disabilities. The former has been well documented for a number of years (Disablement Income Group, 1974, 1979, 1987, Disability Alliance, 1975, 1987), but very little attention has been paid to the disadvantaged position of women with disabilities in relation to social security.

Comprehensive disability income

Because of the anomalies and inequalities in the system of disability benefits, women are severely disadvantaged and one person who is disabled will be better off than another even though both may be in exactly the same circumstances. As a consequence of this a growing demand has been voiced by certain disability organisations for an alternative system of income support for people with disabilities (Disability Alliance, 1987; Disablement Income Group, 1987). In essence the proposal is that most forms of income maintenance for people with disabilities should be replaced by a new benefit variously called a 'national disability income' or a 'comprehensive disability income'. This new benefit will have two parts to it. The first part would be an *allowance* that would be universally available to all people with disabilities regardless of their sex, status or income. It would be paid purely on the basis of a person's disability (rather like Child Benefit, which is paid purely on the basis of having a child) and would, therefore, be a universal benefit which would be relatively easy and cheap to administer. The purpose of this part of the benefit would be to meet the additional daily expenses that are incurred through disability that were outlined above. It could be based on the severity of disability, in recognition of the additional costs that severity brings, to assist in providing a means, through money, of overcoming these costs (the Disability Alliance proposals recommend five rates according to severity).

The second part of a comprehensive disability income scheme would be a *disablement pension*, which would be paid to those people who cannot work in paid employment because of a long-term sickness or disability. It would provide an alternative to earnings just as the Invalidity Pension does at present, but it would not be contribution-based because this discriminates against people in irregular employment, unskilled workers, and women, but would be paid solely on the basis of incapacity for work.

The dilemma this kind of proposal gives rise to, is that while it would be an advantage to some groups of people, it would simultaneously disadvantage others. In any process of levelling like this, people currently receiving small amounts of benefits (who tend to be women, people disabled early on in life, and immigrants who are ineligible for certain benefits) will gain, while those receiving more generous amounts (who tend to be men, war pensioners and industrial injury pensioners) will stand to have their benefit reduced. The cost of increasing all benefits up to the highest level has inhibited the introduction of such a policy. Nonetheless, the proposal for a single, integrated, non-means-tested benefit has wide support in Britain, including support from the independent Social Security Advisory Committee and all the political parties except the Conservative Party. The group who would undoubtedly benefit most from the introduction of such a scheme would be women, as the above discussion on their situation *vis-à-vis* social security shows.

Partial incapacity benefit

There has also been some support for a 'partial incapacity benefit' for those individuals who are able to do some paid work but whose earning capacity is affected by their disability. This issue has been a long-standing concern of the Multiple Sclerosis Society and Nicole Davoud, the founder member of its youth group. Part-time employment is an attractive option to many young adults who have developed multiple sclerosis and who have a full working life still ahead of them. It is an option which also finds favour among other individuals as a form of employment which can accommodate the needs of someone with a degenerative illness. As outlined in Chapter 7, however, the only way someone with a disability in Britain can at present combine paid work and the receipt of social security is through a limited and strictly controlled form of therapeutic earnings.

There have been a number of proposals for a change in this policy. The Multiple Sclerosis Society proposed a new scheme based on modifying the therapeutic earnings limit into an earnings rule. In 1983 the Social Security Advisory Committee put forward two proposals as a way forward towards the introduction of a partial incapacity benefit. The simplest one was called 'disablement income supplement'. This would provide a benefit graduated according to earnings and family responsibilities, and would be payable for a fixed period of time regardless of changes in circumstances. People claiming it would have to work a minimum number of hours a week and would have to show a medical certificate from their own general practitioner to say that their disability had materially affected their earning capacity.

The other option was called 'partial incapacity pension', although it has elements of the costs allowance referred to above. Instead of eligibility being determined mainly by reference to earning capacity, it would be decided by a test of severity of disability on the assumption that anyone who was severely disabled would have both lower earnings and extra working expenses than a non-disabled counterpart. The benefit would be flat-rate and subject to an earnings rule, with a tapered reduction on earnings initially, followed by a pound-for-pound reduction thereafter. Although the second option is the more expensive and difficult to administer, it might well be a better one for women. Because eligibility is determined by severity of disability rather than earning capacity, it is open to fewer assumptions being made about women's legitimacy in the labour market or their potential earnings. Nonetheless, it is difficult to avoid the conclusion that any partial benefit would be of particular help to the much higher proportions of women with disabilities such as multiple sclerosis and arthritis, for whom part-time work is so essential.

Wealth accumulation

Income from earnings or social security benefits are not the only means by which people make a living. Income from sources other than earnings and benefits for people with disabilities most commonly tend to be pensions or redundancy payments, but also include income from savings or investments. These tend to be very small amounts of income. For instance, 18 per cent of non-pensioners receive some income from the former, averaging £38.70 net per week, while 20 per cent of non-pensioners receive some income from the latter, averaging £19.00 net per week (Martin and White, 1988). People also sometimes obtain an income from assets or other forms of wealth. Wealth can be accumulated in a number of ways. Some of the less spectacular, but nonetheless lucrative, ways for ordinary people are owning a home, taking out insurance, and being a member of an occupational pension scheme. All three are more difficult for women, especially if they have a disability. However, all are ways of avoiding the poverty that so often accompanies old age – with which many women with disabilities are justifiably concerned.

There are distinct financial advantages to owning a home. It is an investment which usually appreciates in value, sometimes considerably. It is an asset which protects against inflation, and it is generously subsidised through the tax system in Britain. The high cost of housing, however, makes it a substantial capital investment and constrains access to ownership. Most people who wish to buy a house must be in a position to obtain a loan in order to do so. The lending policies of institutions in the mortgage market take into account the characteristics of the potential borrowers, ostensibly to protect the interest of their investors. The result of this is that certain groups find it more difficult to obtain loans. These are likely to be people who do not have a steady income or whose attachment to the labour force is tenuous, such as women and people with disabilities (Buckle, 1971).

In the light of the earlier evidence presented of the high rates of unemployment and the low incomes of women with disabilities, it is far less likely that they will own their own homes. In the 1988 OPCS study, fewer disabled than non-disabled adults owned their own home, particularly those of working age. This confirmed the earlier OPCS study in 1969, which also found that fewer non-married women were owner-occupiers. Single women and widows tended to be in private rented accommodation (Buckle, 1971, pp. 67, 130; Martin and White, 1988). They are even less likely to be owner-occupiers if they are working-class women or women living with working-class men, as only 21 per cent of unskilled manual workers own their own homes, compared to 85 per cent of professional people (Burke, 1981, p. 42). As shown in Chapter 7, women with disabilities are least likely to be professionals and most likely to be unskilled workers compared to all men and non-disabled women.

People who have to give up paid employment because of ill-health may be able to resort to extended sick pay arrangements with their employers or an early retirement pension or, more recently, be eligible for Permanent Health Insurance (PHI). In all three cases, women are treated differently to men. Fewer women have access to occupational sick pay schemes, particularly if they are manual workers (Lonsdale and Byrne, 1988). Only 35 per cent of women were in occupational pension schemes in 1979, compared to 63 per cent of men. To a large extent this is due to the common practice of excluding part-time workers from such schemes (Brown and Small, 1985, p. 164). This becomes important for women who are disabled because they may be more likely to be in part-time work, but also because the availability of ill-health or early retirement pensions usually depends on membership of an occupational pension scheme (although not all include such provisions).

Even if a woman qualifies for an ill-health pension, certain things may lessen the amount of money she will receive from it. First, broken career patterns characterise women's employment and make the accumulation of pension entitlements more difficult. If a women has any preserved pension rights these may be further reduced if she becomes disabled when not actually in employment. Second, lower wages lessen the value of pension rights, and since women tend to be low paid, they will be more vulnerable to this.

There has been only one detailed study of occupational pension scheme provision for people with disabilities, and it reported few restrictions (Occupational Pensions Board, 1977). This was partly because the pooling of good and bad risks was cheap and cost-effective to administer, so non-discrimination was to the advantage of the scheme (Ward, 1986). However, some concern was expressed that employers would use pension schemes as an excuse not to hire people with disabilities, a concern found also in a study of over 1,200 people with multiple sclerosis (Davoud and Kettle, 1980, p. 45).

Permanent health insurance is another means of insuring against disability. It has grown slowly in recent years, with only one and a half million people being covered by 1982 (Brown and Small, 1985, p. 97). Those covered tended to be directors and managers. This is partly because there is a greater risk of ill-health among manual workers who are, therefore, less likely to be accepted into such schemes. There is also an in-built deterrence against the coverage of women. Insurance companies charge women 50 per cent more than men for permanent health insurance because they believe that women have that much higher an incidence of ill-health than men, although the data used to arrive at this conclusion are under dispute. In 1986, a case was taken to court under the Sex Discrimination Act, but the practice was found to be legal and the data used, reasonable

(Brown and Small, 1985, p. 235; Ward, 1986). This puts women who become disabled at an extreme disadvantage. However, permanent health insurance is valuable as a form of extended sick pay and protects people from having to leave the labour market prematurely. Given the status and legitimacy of women in the labour force, this may be an important source of protection for some.

The above discussion shows how especially vulnerable women are to poverty. This has to be understood in relation to the particular lack of access which women have to three things: well-paid jobs, adequate social security benefits, and the processes of wealth generation, i.e. the 'principal resource systems of society' (Townsend, 1979; Glendinning and Millar, 1987). For women who are disabled, access to these means of independence and self-support is limited in different ways and to a greater extent than it is for most other people.

9

Discrimination and civil rights

It has been illustrated thus far that there is more to physical disability than having a body which is atypical or does not function as well as it might. Having a physical disability means living in society as a minority group whose particular needs are not adequately recognised or taken into account, and whose different appearance often leads to being treated differently and less equally. This usually means being at greater risk of poverty and exclusion, as previous chapters have shown, alongside other minority groups. Disability, like race and sex, is not a matter of choice, but arises from birth or disease or trauma. The impact it has on the life of an individual often results as much from the physical progression of the disability as the way in which that person is defined and treated by the society in which he or she lives.

For the non-disabled, the disability may represent the most dominant and important element of that person's make-up, whereas for the person *with* the disability, it is often simply a fact of life, one characteristic among many, and not necessarily the most decisive or influential in their choice of action. On another level, like race and gender, disability is a political entity because negative attitudes towards the disability are often generalised to other characteristics of the person concerned. The process which ensues can ultimately lead to an overall state of subordination and social disadvantage.

There is a curious contradiction in the behaviour and attitudes of many able-bodied people towards disability. Some recent surveys of public attitudes towards people with disabilities have shown a remarkable degree of support for policies which are aimed at assisting people who are disabled, even if such policies incur a public cost (OUTSET, 1987a; Weir, 1981). One study undertaken by MORI in 1987 (when public expenditure restraint had become the accepted conventional wisdom for a healthy economy) found that 71 per cent of the electorate (including the same proportion of Conservative voters) thought that additional funding should be made available by central government for creating more employment opportunities for people with disabilities. The same proportion felt that extra financial support should be given to enable disabled people to live independently in the community. Ninety per cent thought that all forms of public transport should be legally obliged to be accessible to people with disabilities. Conservative voters in particular were in favour of funding for greater accessibility in the form of things like wider corridors, special seating, ramps, improved signs, changing floor textures for people with visual disabilities, and more and clearer announcements on railway platforms. With regard to education, 78 per cent of the electorate felt that children with physical disabilities should go to ordinary schools (OUTSET, 1987a).

In January of the same year Gallup interviewed a nationally representative sample of over 1,000 adults in Britain on their attitudes to the incomes of people with disabilities. The results showed that a majority of people not only believed there were inequalities in the social security system for people with disabilities, but were prepared to pay for a national disability income. The majority of respondents thought that the level of most social security disability benefits (excluding industrial injuries benefits) were 'completely inadequate'. In the case of Severe Disablement Allowance, 83 per cent of the sample thought this was 'completely inadequate'. In the light of this, 67 per cent were prepared to pay an additional amount of tax to cover the costs of improving the incomes of people with disabilities (Thompson, 1987).

Given the extraordinary consensus expressed by voters of all political persuasions that policy should move in these directions, it is somewhat surprising to find that the public does not live up to the generosity that studies like these would lead one to expect. The extent to which people with disabilities encounter prejudicial attitudes from the public is probably not generally recognised, yet many studies include accounts of hurtful, offensive incidents.

Although most come from ignorance, naivety or fear on the part of the perpetrators, this makes them no less painful encounters.

Attitudes towards disability

In the present study, a number of women mentioned incidents that had occurred on social occasions which had upset or irritated them at the time, and had had a deterrent effect on going out in the long term. For instance, Enid told of being stopped when going into a shop one day because the owner felt that her wheelchair would damage the furniture. Another woman described the following incident, which she said was not uncommon:

> I went to the Ideal Homes exhibition, and this horrible woman with a dog crashed into my chair and she said, 'You shouldn't be allowed in here.' My friend said, 'You shouldn't be allowed in here with your silly little dog.' People can be rude sometimes.

Swasti, a gregarious young woman in her early twenties who said she very much enjoyed going out and who liked to lead a social life, referred to ordinary, everyday incidents which she found hurtful:

> Sometimes, if you go shopping and you have to stop because it's crowded, people walk right across you. Sometimes you can't stop fast enough not to hit their legs, and they give you such a dirty look. You say sorry, and you know it's not your fault.

Negative and hostile encounters with members of the public were expressed more often by younger women in this study. This may be due to its being a new experience for them, as well as the importance that social contacts have for older adolescents. Public attitudes of staring at someone with a disability contrasted, for some women, with being ignored or not being looked at when they were talking to able-bodied people. Most of the women interviewed remarked on the humiliation of people talking to their able-bodied friends or companions as if they would not be able to understand what was being said. Shantu recounted a number of incidences of being stared at. She lives with her extended family and often looks after her nieces and nephews, but is made to feel that there is something wrong with her behaving like a normal aunt:

> If I go out shopping with the children, the looks you get, or the comments – 'I
> wouldn't let my child go out with her like that.' That hurts. As if the child is in
> some sort of danger. But the looks I get with my car when I have the kids with me
> in it! And taking my chair out of the car, some people will just stand and stare and
> watch me do it. I just ignore people like that, who just stare.

There were some rather more extreme examples of invasion of
privacy, such as Sheila's experience of having been blessed in public
by a complete stranger! Carole also mentioned rather wryly that she
had had a stranger come up to her in the High Street one Saturday
morning and give her ten pence.

Some women felt that public attitudes towards them and the
response they got from people improved if they were well-dressed or
if they were sitting down. Ironically, one woman who had
encountered racism, felt that attitudes improved when she wore
her sari. This may have been due to the sari obscuring her disability,
particularly since all the black women interviewed said that their
disability was a greater handicap than their colour. Debra, who
generally had to move by using a wheelchair but who could still
stand, said she felt other people's attitudes were completely different
towards her when she was sitting than when she was standing. While
others seemed to feel more comfortable and at ease with her when
she was sitting in her wheelchair, she felt less patronised and more
assertive when standing.

There is often an assumption of dependence on the part of people
who have a disability. The assumption of dependency can take the
form of trying to be helpful without being asked and, in doing so,
invading the privacy of the disabled person's life, as Enid described
the following incident:

> Another time, I tried to go and see the Leonardo da Vinci cartoons at the Royal
> Academy. We drove into London, found a parking place and all that palaver.
> There was a huge queue, and this terrible man ran out, grabbed my wheelchair and
> said, 'Mind out for the wheelchair.' I would have been quite prepared to queue. He
> shoved us right up to the front. We got in, and the head person in charge said, 'Oh,
> wheelchairs were yesterday.' And I wasn't politically aware enough to fight him.
> He wouldn't let me in to see them. And I've never ever gone back there, I really
> should have written a letter of protest. Now, I would.

Aside from this woman being referred to as a 'wheelchair', it is
interesting to speculate what the general reaction would have been
had a non-disabled woman been so unceremoniously grabbed and

propelled to the front of the queue, or had she protested at his behaviour. In the former situation, it is quite likely that public anger or disapproval would have been directed at the man, while in the latter, it is likely to have been directed to the 'ungracious' woman in the wheelchair.

A number of women had been on the receiving end of careless and thoughtless behaviour which they had found particularly hurtful. These usually entailed being excluded from social events by friends or family. One young adolescent said her family did not mind saying that she couldn't come with them on a family outing to friends' houses when these houses were inaccessible to her. Another young student had been excluded from most social events at college, as she describes:

> . . . the senior common room was upstairs, and that's where the social events were held. Out of pride my friend and I wouldn't go. We were annoyed; they knew we were around but they still held them upstairs. There was a room downstairs where they could do it. So, we couldn't meet people there either. We asked them plenty of times to hold them downstairs. They said they would, but they didn't. They forgot. You give in in the end.

One story which was recounted suggests that as in all cases of prejudice and discrimination, people make exceptions for individuals while still holding their prejudices against the group as a whole:

> I think it's harder for women with disability. I've known someone, we've been friends for years, we can talk about anything. We go back from when we were at school. And he has recently met X [a friend who is also physically disabled]. We went to her party, and when we got there, he said to me, 'It's suddenly dawned on me, is your friend in a wheelchair?' I said, yes. And that took him totally by surprise. He said, 'You didn't tell me that your friend was in a wheelchair,' I said, does it matter? He said, 'No it doesn't, but I'm so used to all your friends being able-bodied, that I never thought of you having friends who are disabled.' He said, 'I'm not staying here at this party.' I thought he was kidding, but he was quite serious. When we went in, he was really uneasy. X picked it up as well. I suppose she has come into contact with it more than I have.

Fortunately, the story had an outcome which led to greater understanding all round:

> He started talking to a guy who was disabled, and they hit it off really well. They were in the same kind of profession, they exchanged addresses and phone numbers, and they found they could help each other with their work. And he came away

having totally enjoyed the party. And he goes round to see X quite often. All the years that he has known me, which must be about fifteen years, since meeting X he has learned more about me than before.

As these examples show, discrimination occurs at many different levels, ranging from hostility and aggression to patronage, exclusion and fear. At worst, it is manifested in acts of aggression towards members of the discriminated group or minority (Titley and Viney, 1969). It most commonly takes the form of excluding individuals from employment, education and places of leisure and social interaction (CORAD, 1982, Spastics Society, 1985; 1986). It can also be said to exist by default when certain facilities are unavailable for specific groups, contributing to a loss of normal independence or segregation, such as adapted housing or accessible transport for people with disabilities (Shelter, 1988).

Legally, discrimination has a more precise definition, although in Britain it only covers women and ethnic minorities. Here, discrimination can be direct or indirect. Section 1(1) of the Sex Discrimination Act says that 'a person discriminates against a woman in any circumstances relevant for the purposes of the Act if – (a) on the ground of her sex, he treats her less favourably than a man'. Similarly, Section 1(1)(a) of the Race Relations Act says that a person discriminates against another if 'on racial grounds he treats that other less favourable than he treats or would treat other persons'.

Indirect discrimination is also covered by these two Acts, but it is a more complex legal concept. It is also designed to have a wider impact than direct discrimination in recognising and dealing with apparently neutral situations which have a disproportionate effect on a particular group such as women, e.g. recruitment or selection criteria which are deemed to be not essential to a job, but which make it difficult or impossible for some groups to apply. In both the Sex Discrimination Act and the Race Relations Act, indirect discrimination is similarly defined. In the latter, it is where someone applies a requirement or condition which applies equally to people of different racial groups, but:

(i) which is such that the proportion of persons of the same racial group as that other who can comply with it is considerably smaller than the proportion of persons not of that racial group who can comply with it; and

(ii) which he cannot show to be justifiable irrespective of the colour, race, nationality, or ethnic or national origins of the person to whom it is applied; and

(iii) which is to the detriment of that other because he cannot comply with it. (Section 1(1)(b), quoted in Palmer and Poulton, 1987.)

Whereas the *intention* behind certain actions is important in direct discrimination, the *effect* of certain actions is important in indirect discrimination. Anti-discrimination legislation such as these represent attempts to make it illegal and, therefore, to stop grounds for choice being based on sex or race. Since there is no similar legislation for people with disabilities, there is no legal constraint stopping employers from taking disability into account when recruiting for jobs or deciding on promotions. Likewise there are no legal constraints on disabled people being excluded from a wide variety of activities.

Lack of access

One of the greatest forms of discrimination which many people with disabilities face is having lack of access to buildings and functions. Obviously, this is a more serious problem for someone with severely restricted mobility. It becomes even more serious when someone's civil rights are at stake. One disabled woman who is active in politics expressed concern that some of the buildings she had been to for district elections were inaccessible, threatening some people's ability to vote. The inaccessibility of some public services such as employment offices, social security offices, job centres, social services departments and Town Halls is well known. One woman said that in her area, her benefit office, library, police station and job centre were all inaccessible to her in her wheelchair, severely curtailing her rights and the life she could choose to lead. A deaf woman felt that her civil rights were being infringed by the fact that her language, i.e. signing, was not given legal recognition.

In addition, the form summonsing people to jury service in England includes the following footnote: 'When you attend at court you may be discharged if there is doubt as to your capacity to serve on a jury because of physical disability or insufficient understanding of English.' This statement is not clarified, and it is therefore questionable whether, for instance, the incapacity of a courthouse to accommodate a wheelchair might be used as a reason for discharging a potential juror who is a wheelchair user. It is also questionable whether the language of a deaf person would be considered to have legitimacy in an English court.

There is growing evidence of discrimination towards people with disabilities due to the inaccessibility of many places, which results in their exclusion from those places ... This was recognised officially in 1979 when the then Labour government set up a Committee on Restrictions against Disabled People (CORAD) with a brief to 'consider the architectural and social barriers which may result in discrimination against disabled people and prevent them making full use of facilities available to the general public, and to make recommendations'. Among other things, the Committee looked at access to buildings, public transport, employment, education, and the impact of fire and safety regulations. It attempted to find out the extent of discrimination in those areas by use of a questionnaire sent to an unusually large number of individuals. Discrimination was found to be particularly high in employment. However, the largest number of people voiced problems related to the inaccessibility of buildings. CORAD submitted its report in May 1982 to a new Conservative government, which did not accept that the discrimination found was widespread enough to warrant legislation.

Perhaps the most serious infringement of the civil rights of some people with disabilities is the poor access to polling stations and booths during general and local elections. People with disabilities represent 13 per cent of the electorate yet face the possibility of disenfranchisement because of this lack of access. Section 18 of the Representation of the People Act 1983 places an obligation on district borough councils and London boroughs to designate, as far as is reasonable and practicable, only places which are accessible as polling stations. Home Office guidance is that this must be a long-term objective. Grants are available to adapt buildings to make them accessible. However, prior to the 1987 general election, the Spastics Society undertook a study in five representative constituencies and found widespread evidence of people who did not vote because of the difficulties of getting to a polling station and because they felt that postal or proxy voting was discriminatory.

Subsequent to the CORAD report, the Spastics Society (1985, 1986) published two reports documenting evidence of discrimination against people with disabilities. The first detailed forty-six cases of discrimination collected by a group of voluntary organisations. Some included relatively clear cases of direct discrimination, such as a pub refusing to serve someone a drink solely on account of their being disabled. Others included cases of indirect discrimination. One such case was that of a blind woman being unable to enter the Stranger's Gallery in the House of Commons because there was no facility for her guide dog. In another, a woman was refused a job because her disability made it necessary for her to wear trousers, and the firm required that female employees should wear skirts. Perhaps surprisingly, the report was prepared to exclude some cases of alleged discrimination such as when a private health insurance company refused cover for treatment arising out of deafness, on the basis that this might have involved the company in a disproportionate cost.

Places of public entertainment are legally entitled to exclude people with disabilities, and they sometimes do. Carole, a young nineteen-year-old, had not been allowed in to a disco, and had also experienced being asked to leave a pub. She believed both these incidents had had nothing to do with access or safety regulations, but were based on negative attitudes towards her being disabled:

> Obviously attitudes are the first things I would like to see conquered. Because these big night clubs, they think it's going to ruin their image if there's people with disabilities in there. Clubs like the . . . and the discos, they don't allow people in. Personally, I don't think it's the access problem. I think it's that they are going to worry about the other customers being offended by people with disabilities.

Since both places are open to the public, people who were excluded on the basis of their race or sex would have recourse under the Race Relations Act or the Sex Discrimination Act. People with disabilities have no such redress, as there is no similar legislation which covers them. By contrast, private clubs are legally entitled to exclude individuals on any basis. The section of the Sex Discrimination Act dealing with the provision of goods, facilities and services is limited to the public sphere. Even the European Court of Justice, while criticising the generalised way in which private clubs did exclude women, stated that it accepted the exclusion of private clubs from the legislation because the intention of the exclusion was 'to reconcile the principle of equality of treatment with the principle of respect for private life which is also fundamental' (O'Donovan and

Szyszczak, 1988, p. 81). However, the rights of disabled people are still at the starting post, since there is no legislation at all.

Employment

The second report published by the Spastics Society focused on discrimination in employment. Following a particular tradition in studies of discrimination, fictional paired applications were sent off for 152 jobs. For each job the two applicants had equivalent experience of education and work and were of the same age and sex. One specified that he or she had a disability. An interview, a request to telephone, and sending the applicant an application form were all considered to be positive responses by employers. Ninety-three of the tests were valid in that they contained at least one positive response. In 41 per cent of cases, only the disabled candidate received a negative response. In 3 per cent of cases, only the able-bodied candidate did. The results showed a statistically significant indication of discrimination against people with a disability – at a very early stage in the job selection procedure.

The study also analysed the negative responses from the employers. They tended not to give a reason for the decision. In certain cases, however, disabled applicants were told that their qualifications and experience were not appropriate to the job, or that the position had already been filled, at the same time that their able-bodied counterparts had been called for an interview. These covert forms of discrimination are extremely difficult to prove outside of a test setting.

In the present study, some women had come across attitudes which either assumed they were incapable of being employed or that they did not have a right to jobs in short supply. For instance, one woman said she was often asked the question, '*Do* you work?' rather than '*Where* do you work?', although this could be a more general issue in relation to women. Another woman had not experienced discrimination from her employer, but from her fellow workers. She felt that her right to work had been under question:

I had a lot of problems in the civil service, people discriminating against me. Twelve months. In the end, I resigned purely because of the pressure I was under. I was working in a room not much bigger than this. There was me and this other woman. She had never worked with a disabled person before and she was quite old. But she didn't want me to get the job, I think she was frightened. She thought I was taking an able-bodied person's job. She said that. In the civil service, they write reports on you every six months. It's graded in boxes, one to six. One was the top and six the lowest. She gave me a six straight away. That was her way of trying to get me out.

Views on the eligibility of women with disabilities having paid employment are not always expressed outright, and they are easier to deal with in some situations than others. This same woman felt that she came across similar views in another job:

Some of the clerical workers there wouldn't speak to me. They thought a disabled person shouldn't be allowed to work there, in an able-bodied person's job. But, the difference here was – in the other one it was the management who were making the difficulties. In this one, the management were on my side and it was just my other colleagues. And because I knew they couldn't get rid of me, it made it easier for me to battle it. It was a minority of the whole office, but because of the careers officers being out most of the time, it was only the clerical staff who were in, so I was with them all the time.

Anti-discrimination legislation

The conclusion drawn by both CORAD and the Spastics Society was that the rights of people with disabilities in the face of this kind of discrimination could be safeguarded and enforced by the introduction of anti-discrimination legislation. Since the publication of the CORAD Report in 1982, there have been five parliamentary attempts to introduce such legislation in Britain.

The first, in 1982, was a 'ten-minute' Bill, the Disablement (Prohibition of Unjustifiable Discrimination) Bill introduced by Jack Ashley, a long-time campaigner for the rights of people with disabilities and himself a disabled Member of Parliament. The purpose of the Bill was to draw attention to the issue, but it did not make the end of that parliamentary session. Towards the beginning of the following year, another Member of Parliament, Donald Stewart, introduced a Private Member's Bill under the same title. It fell due to a lack of a quorum in the vote on whether to give it a second reading, although there were no votes against it. In November of the same year, the most important parliamentary initiative thus far took place. Robert Wareing MP introduced another Private Member's Bill, the Chronically Sick and Disabled Persons (Amendment) Bill, which had all-party support. The aims of this Bill were to outlaw discrimination on the grounds of physical, mental or sensory disability, to establish a commission to oversee this, and to promote the integration of people with disabilities fully into society, as well as to investigate individual complaints under the Act. The model was clearly that of the existing Race Relations and Sex Discrimination Acts. The Bill covered a wide range of areas, including employment, housing and occupational pension schemes. It was defeated, however, by an unofficial government whip by 210 votes to 164, although this led to some unfavourable publicity against the government.

An attempt was made by Lord Longford to reintroduce the Bill in the House of Lords in 1984. Although amendments were made to it, it was still defeated. Lord Campbell of Croy simultaneously tried to introduce a Bill to investigate allegations of discrimination without making it illegal. This was unopposed in its third reading, but was taken no further.

As well as giving individuals protection against discrimination, this kind of legislation can be argued to have another consequence. The disabled population is an aggregation of diverse individuals of different ages and interests, and with different social and economic backgrounds. This often means they appear to lack any cohesion or identity as a social grouping, especially since their impairments and disabilities are also diverse. However, they have something in common which is so powerful that it has the potential to supersede all differences – exclusion and discrimination on the basis of a physiological difference from the majority population. The oppression that emanates from this exclusion has often been justified on the basis of biological theories of weakness and inferiority, just as it has been for women and racial minorities. Impairment, like gender and race, has been used to explain and justify social disadvantage. The significance of anti-discrimination legislation is political as well as legal, in that it highlights the common ground between people with disabilities. In this, it is a first step to breaking down oppression while also giving individual protection.

The United States has a longer and more successful history of attempting to outlaw discrimination. In 1973 the Rehabilitation Act was passed. This was the first major civil rights legislation for people who are disabled, since it is not only concerned with services and benefits, but also the civil rights of people with disabilities. This is largely on account of Section 504 of the Act, which states that 'no otherwise qualified handicapped individual . . . shall, solely by reason of his or her handicap, be excluded from participation in, be denied the benefits of, or be subject to discrimination under any program or activity receiving Federal financial assistance'. The strength and effectiveness of legislation which not only prohibits discrimination but also attaches a financial penalty to it cannot be underestimated. Section 504 denied federal money to any organisation or programme which discriminated against people on the basis of either physical or mental handicap.

Although the Act was passed in 1973, it took four years for the regulations permitting its full implementation to be signed. The aspect of the legislation which was most disturbing to politicians, thus delaying the signing, was Section 504. Ironically this section had originally been included as a routine matter, almost more of a symbolic gesture towards equal opportunities. In the years following the legislation's enactment, however, it had a significant effect on a number of federal programmes. Those who had understood the significance of Section 504 from the beginning were those for whom it would have the most importance, namely people with disabilities. Growing numbers of disabled people banded together from 1973 to insist on the full implementation of the Act. They organised a nationwide protest movement and protest rallies in selected cities to draw attention to the issue. They lobbied members of Congress and agitated for the signing of the regulations to make the Act fully operational. These actions culminated in the longest sit-in involving federal buildings in the history of the USA and led to the final signing of the regulations.

Despite the strength of the Rehabilitation Act, it nonetheless only applied to federally funded programmes. Consequently, in 1988 the Americans with Disabilities Act 1988 was passed, which will redress the neglect of people with disabilities in the Civil Rights legislation of 1964. It was introduced by four senators, of both Republican and Democratic persuasions. It is one comprehensive piece of legislation that affects all areas of the lives of disabled people. It prohibits discrimination in employment, housing, travel, and state and local government services. Discrimination, whether intentional or not, will now be addressed by law. Unlike the Rehabilitation Act 1973, which only provided protection against discrimination in federally funded programmes, the private sector and local public agencies will now be covered. Unlike the United Kingdom, people with disabilities will receive from the law a good measure of protection against discrimination.

10

Independence and self-determination

Independent living is a freedom of choice to live where and how one chooses and can afford. It is living within the community, in the neighbourhood one chooses. It is living alone or with a room mate of one's choice. It is deciding one's own pattern of life, schedule, food, entertainment, vices, virtues, and friends. It is freedom to take risks and freedom to make mistakes. It is freedom to learn to live independently by living independently. (Derbyshire Coalition of Disabled People, 1985).

Independence and self-determination are only possible when people are able to make choices about how they wish to live their lives, and have the confidence, power and economic means to follow those choices through. People with disabilities have had their choices circumscribed in a number of different ways. The particular constraints women with physical disabilities confront have been described in the preceding chapters. As women, they have been encouraged to be less assertive and more dependent, and to concentrate their energy and priorities on physical appearance, at times to the detriment of their health and well-being. They have often been devalued, and many have internalised negative images of themselves which have constrained their actions. Many have not received the rehabilitation and training necessary to equip them to enter the labour market on equal terms to others. If in paid employment, they frequently experience discrimination and have fewer opportunities to progress in a chosen career. When not in paid work, they have experienced a history of second-rate treatment as applicants and claimants of social security. Women with disabilities, therefore, stand to gain considerably from a politics of disability that will liberate them from these fetters. Such a politics of disability, however, must be one which hears the voices of women, and acknowledges and deals with the particular oppression that women with disabilities experience.

The general movement by people with disabilities towards greater integration into mainstream society and greater control over their own destinies has become embodied in the Independent Living Movement. In the early 1970s the civil rights movement in the United States was extended to include people with disabilities as another minority group who had been excluded and ignored in American society. Section 504 of the Rehabilitation Act 1973 became the first piece of civil rights legislation covering disability.

Spurred on by the black civil rights movement in the USA, the anger of people with disabilities about their treatment slowly grew into a mass disability rights movement. At about the same time in Britain, a similar consciousness of oppression was developing as people with disabilities joined together to lobby for legislation that would recognise their rights to housing and access to buildings, income and support services. In the United States, the disability rights movement culminated in the Rehabilitation Act. In Britain, it resulted in the Chronically Sick and Disabled Persons Act. Both were hailed as milestones in the struggle for independence, although they were very different pieces of legislation; with time, the limitations of both as instruments of policy have become more obvious.

The Rehabilitation Act only covered federally supported programmes, leaving individuals with no redress against discrimination in many situations. It also received a severe setback from a Supreme Court ruling on what had been felt to be the most powerful clause in the Act, Section 504 (in *South East College* v. *Davis*), which judged that a severe hearing loss constituted legitimate grounds for refusal to admit a woman into a nurse's training course (Shearer, 1981, p. 186). To a much greater extent, the Chronically Sick and Disabled Persons Act has proved over the years to be inadequate in identifying need and providing services. It is based on a philosophy which is in almost complete opposition to that of the Rehabilitation Act. It is concerned with *needs* not *rights*, and with the provision of welfare facilities rather than offering a mechanism to fight discrimination.

Nonetheless, both Acts provided an impetus to action, even if it was on the basis of what policy should *not* look like. The Independent Living Movement became the more positive focal point around which many disabled women and men began to organise. In 1972, the first Centre for Independent Living (CIL) was established in Berkeley, California, and its overall purpose was to assist people with disabilities to identify and meet their own needs. Fundamental to its philosophy and organisation was the policy that the Centre should be managed and run by people who were disabled themselves. It aimed to transform people from being passive recipients of services controlled by others to being actively involved in determining not only what services they wanted but how they wished to obtain them. It was to be based on peer group support and help. In the United States, every CIL is by law required to have at least 51 per cent of people with disabilities on its board. The names 'Centre for Independent Living' and 'CIL' are registered trademarks, and as such cannot be used by other people (Derbyshire Coalition of Disabled People, 1985, p. 8).

Today there are approximately two hundred CILs in the United States. In Britain, there are seven at various stages of development – in Derbyshire, Hampshire, Greenwich, Southampton, Nottingham, Strathclyde, and Milton Keynes. Like most CILs, they are non-residential and are fiercely committed to being run by people with disabilities. The largest is the Derbyshire CIL, which to a limited extent involves people who are not disabled and, therefore, calls itself a Centre for *Integrated* Living. The reason for this approach must be seen in the political context in which the Centre found itself. It did not wish to lend credence to those who ostensibly extol self-help while welcoming such schemes as a means of withdrawing state assistance and finance from them. But it wished to reject the paternalism that has traditionally accompanied welfare provision. Therefore, the Centre works with and expects local authority financing, at the same time as requiring independence in decision-making. It appears to be successfully steering a course between working with the local authority that finances it and retaining ultimate control over its own destiny. The key to its success seems to be the coalition of disabled people who have negotiated firm terms and conditions under which it is prepared to work with people who are not disabled (Derbyshire Coalition of Disabled People, 1985).

The development of CILs has been linked to the growth of new types of organisations which stress that they are organisations *of* disabled people rather than organisations *for* disabled people. Traditionally, the provision of services has been within the welfare model of agencies run by people who are not disabled and who determine not only the type of service on offer, but what the needs are of disabled people. Although some agencies devolved more power to their consumer group than others, there was still a strong feeling in some quarters that until those consumers controlled the agency, people with disabilities would never satisfactorily receive the services they wanted. Moreover, controlling services was seen to be an important part in the process of personal growth away from the helpless, dependent and subservient role which many people with disabilities felt they had been socialised to play. It was also a means to making disability more visible. Nicole Davoud, in her history of involvement with the Multiple Sclerosis Society, describes this as follows:

> There was a crying need for disabled people to do things for themselves and by themselves. If our campaign for integration and participation was to have any meaning, we had to become our own spokes [persons]. This meant that in a way disabled people themselves had to change the perception that they had of their own capabilities. They had been downtrodden and ignored for so long that they had lost their sense of identity and self-respect. Disabled people had to be seen to be fighting and occupying places of note, be on all the committees dealing with disabled people. I wanted the involvement of the media not just with documentaries about what it means to be disabled, but I wanted disabled people to be invited to attend panel games and do the same sort of things that able-bodied people do.

The British Council of Organisations of Disabled People (BCODP) was formed in the 1980s to promote the type of approach whereby disabled people start to become more visible and involved in making policy, in opposition to the other major national disability organisation, the Royal Association for Disability and Rehabilitation (RADAR). It very soon established itself as the antithesis of RADAR in terms of philosophy and organisation, as well as the constituency which it represented. To date, however, RADAR remains the dominant organisation in terms of official recognition and funding. Its government grant is twenty-five times greater than that given to BCODP.

Much of the organising to redefine what the problem of disability was and to change the situation of disabled people, did not initially embrace the particular circumstances and the peculiarly different type of oppression experienced by women who were disabled. To some extent, the problems seem, and often are, the same. Lack of physical access to a public building affects men as much as it does women, although women who are housebound with young children face lack of access of a different kind. Enforced helplessness and dependency is equally damaging to men and women, although it may not be recognised as so damaging to women because of assumptions that women are dependent anyhow. Consequently, articles on the oppression of people with disability that were important to the early disability rights movement would still use sexist language and were dominated by a view of the world that was unashamedly male (Battye, 1966).

The re-emerging feminist movement of the 1960s and 1970s began within a very short space of time to have a considerable impact on the awareness and consciousness of millions of women about their position and status in the world. Some women were influenced directly and immediately. Other women were affected by the changed it wrought, such as less restrictive abortion laws, equal pay laws, the prohibition of sex discrimination, and so on. This powerful movement was to some extent given international recognition by the United Nations Declaration of International Women's Year in 1975 and the subsequent Decade for Women. Within this decade, the International Year of Disabled People (IYDP) was declared in 1981. For a disabled woman, therefore, two of the most integral elements of their lives and their oppression in society were separated out as distinct and unrelated. Interestingly, as Mary Croxon John (1988, p. 12) points out, the original plan for the Decade of Women contained a decision to include a specific focus on women with disabilities, but this was dropped in favour of its being included instead in IYDP.

In the decade since IYDP, women with disabilities have begun organising themselves on a greater scale than hitherto. The Disabled Person's International has a women's committee, some disability organisations have formed women's groups, and groups of women have come together as feminists to explore their situation and work towards improving it. Sisters Against Disablement, for example, has adopted a charter of rights for women with disabilities, equivalent to but different from the demands of the women's movement (Hannaford, 1985).

In many ways, the objectives of the women's movement and groups of disabled women are the same: ending discrimination, developing a consciousness among women of how they are disadvantaged, and attempting to reshape and restructure society along feminist lines. But again, as Mary Croxon John clearly outlines in her study of European women, some of the symbols of combating oppression which the women's movement adopted, such as abortion on demand and a rejection of excessive femininity, have often been considered unacceptable to women with disabilities because they gloss over issues which are crucial to them. Being treated as sexual objects has been a major focus of discontent among many feminists, just as the sexual neutering that is associated with disability has been for many women with disabilities.

The right to *have* children has been the battle of many disabled women, not the right to have an abortion, which has often been only too easy to obtain. Although both represent the same issue, i.e. the control of women's reproduction, abortion did not have the same powerful significance for disabled women as it did for non-disabled women. Or, at least, it had significance as something which had been either imposed on a number of women with disabilities against their will, or was a threat lurking in the background to any woman with a disability who might wish to have a child but who feared being judged as incapable of caring for that child. Similarly, for women whose sexuality has been denied on account of their disability, there has been a different kind of concern about issues relating to excessive treatment of women as sex objects. Again, the issue is the same, i.e. a demand for free and equal treatment that allows each woman to determine the parameters of her own sexuality herself; but the symbols expressing this have not always had the same meaning for women with disabilities as they have for non-disabled women.

Within the women's movement in recent years, differences have been highlighted between the experiences of older and younger women, between those of mothers at home and mothers in paid employment, between women with children and those who are child-free, between disabled and non-disabled women, between lesbians and heterosexual women, and between ordinary working women and professional career women. The challenge for feminism has become one of discovering the links and common experiences between women who, on the surface, appear to have and often feel they have very different lives. At the same time, the disabled women's movement is seeking to define the common issues confronting women with very different types of impairments such as deafness, spinal injury, multiple sclerosis, intellectual impairment, and many others.

Adequate incomes

An adequate income is an important part of independence and self-determination, although these issues clearly extend far beyond financial matters. People with disabilities reflect the more general pattern of inequality that exists in the population as a whole. However, as a minority that experiences discrimination, they are also more vulnerable to poverty and unequal treatment than the majority, as has been shown in earlier chapters. While there may be some individuals with disabilities who are wealthy and powerful, there are a disproportionate number who are poorer and have less power than the majority population. Women generally are also more likely to experience poverty (Glendinning and Millar, 1987). The coalescence of being both disabled and a woman, therefore, poses a considerable likelihood of financial hardship and penury. The issue of a sufficient income through which to express one's preferences and choices is of great importance to women generally, but is especially important to those women whose independence has been further curtailed by the consequences of disability.

Some writers have rightly taken issue with an approach which is narrowly economistic and which equates the problems of disability only with those of poverty, in that it neglects a wider social and political analysis of disability (Oliver, 1984). Denying the significance of income as a major source of inequality in society would be mistaken, however. It would also ignore the significance of poverty among women for whom an adequate income is a crucial part of liberation. The issue of an adequate income is part of a more general one of the distributional systems in our society and the inequalities they both generate and perpetuate.

The two main systems of distribution for most ordinary people in our society are those of employment and earnings on the one hand, and social security payments on the other. In considering the issue of economic resources for people with disabilities, it is important not to restrict consideration to the vexed question of social security provision with its assumptions of dependency. Employment and the right to earn one's own living are important and neglected issues, as all too often it is assumed that people with disabilities will not be able to work in paid employment. However, for many women bringing up children, social security represents their only potential source of income. Focusing on social security in relation to women is not so much a question of dependency, but necessity.

Employment and the right to earn one's living have not been noticeable elements of British policy regarding disability, despite the existence of an employment quota. In many respects, the difficulties that many people with disabilities experience in trying to get suitable paid employment reflect the more general problem of a society which makes assumptions about what individuals can or cannot do on the basis of appearance and stereotypes. People with disabilities have always experienced disproportionately higher rates of unemployment, particularly long-term unemployment. All too often they have been segregated in low-status, badly paid and uninteresting sheltered employment (Lonsdale and Walker, 1984). In addition to the problems of prejudice and discrimination, the search for jobs is often exacerbated by a lack of accompanying facilities such as adequate and appropriate transport, accessible buildings, and the provision of practical domestic support. Consequently, the key distributional system in society is barred to certain groups.

While not all individuals may choose to work (and a woman, whether disabled or not, bringing up small children may be just such a person), such a choice becomes academic in the face of all these constraints. Without paid employment, an individual has fewer social contacts, less status, less power, and, most important, less income. In order to increase the independence and self-determination of people with disabilities, this group must be given a wider choice of ways in which they can be self-supporting. These choices must include not only the right to paid employment if it is desired, but also the right to an income which is sufficient and non-stigmatising. At present, social security is one means by which an income, other than earnings, can be provided to individuals, although most such incomes are far from being sufficient and can be stigmatising.

Social security has a wider significance as well. As was shown in Chapter 8, there are a considerable number of state benefits for people with disabilities, based on different principles and different criteria of eligibility. There is a crude hierarchy of provision between people injured at work or at war, national insurance claimants, non-contributory claimants, and those reliant on means-tested benefits. The system is full of anomalies and inequalities which have two important effects for any political movement concerned with mobilising disabled people to fight for their rights. First they have set up barriers between different groups of disabled people, giving some groups a vested interest in not identifying with others. As a major distributional system, social security in its present form creates a disincentive to collective action by all people with disabilities. Second, as has been shown, the social security system severely disadvantages women. Therefore, they will be the main beneficiaries of a reform which replaces the present anomalous structure with a single integrated and comprehensive benefit.

The Independent Living Fund: charity or specialised help?

The reform of social security which took place in the second half of the 1980s led a number of disability organisations to voice concern over the harsh consequences of the reform for many people with disabilities. In particular, the reforms did away with special weekly additional payments, including some for domestic assistance, on which many people with especially severe disabilities relied. This gave rise to increased campaigning for a comprehensive disability income scheme, as outlined in Chapter 8, and to the launch of a National Campaign for Independence by the Wales Council for the Disabled, who were concerned that poverty would force some disabled people into institutional care against their will.

The government response to such campaigns was to announce the setting up of an independent charitable trust with government funding of 5 million for its first year. The purpose of this trust, named the Independent Living Fund, is to target resources on people who are very severely disabled and who need additional help, domestic and personal, to enable them to live independently in their own homes. The Fund was set up with the co-operation of another charitable organisation, the Disablement Income Group, although it was heavily criticised for doing so by many disability organisations (Large, 1988).

Ten trustees were appointed to execute the Fund and to decide on the criteria for awarding payments to individuals. The biggest concern expressed about the Fund was that it would make payments on the basis of charity rather than as a right to which all people who are disabled are entitled if they are to lead normal independent lives. It was also criticised for not having a statutory right of appeal against decisions made by non-elected and non-representative trustees. It did, however, provide more generous payments than would have been available previously under the old social security system. The Fund offers fewer discretionary but more generous payments to people with severe disabilities, expressing a philosophy of selective targeting of charitable payments in contrast to more universal payments available as of right.

In this, the Fund contrasts sharply with something like the Danish *Århus* scheme, which also has as its aim the provision of financial assistance to enable people who are severely disabled to stay in their own homes. Unlike the Independent Living Fund, the *Århus* scheme is enshrined in mainstream state social security legislation. It is built around a philosophy which stresses the importance of people with disabilities remaining in their own homes rather than institutions, and underwrites costs related to practical assistance as well as care or attendance needs. A condition of eligibility is that the person receiving such assistance must take an active part in negotiating the level of assistance and in the daily administration of the scheme. The scheme is important, therefore, not only in providing support, but also in facilitating self-determination and control on the part of the person who is disabled. The claimants employ their own assistants, and are offered courses in how to be good employers. Although the scheme is costly, it is considered to be less expensive than institutional care (Croxon John, 1988).

A similar experimental scheme was set up in Stockholm in Sweden in 1987 in the form of an independent living co-operative. Instead of using care assistants provided by social services, a sum of money was paid to the co-operative out of which individual members could employ attendants directly themselves. This policy has now spread to people living in a variety of different living circumstances, even those still living in the parental home (Jones, 1987).

In Britain, the provision of attendant care takes the form of both cash benefits to pay for it, and services in kind. The Attendance Allowance scheme is a tax-free benefit which is paid to individuals who need special support and supervision, regardless of whether they are actually in receipt of it. It is aimed at people who are severely disabled and is paid at two rates. Neither rate is sufficient to pay for intensive help, although it does embody the principle that the person with the disability can choose and organise their own care requirements. By contrast, local authority social services do not make payments of this nature and tend to offer services in kind, if they offer any at all. The principle embodied in this approach is that the local authority, or professional employed by it, makes the decision about whether such help is needed and how it will be provided. It locks people with disabilities 'into a service providers' perception of what is good for them', limiting rather than expanding their choices (Shearer, 1981, p. 82). One change from this pattern can be found in Hampshire, where the social services department has found a way of indirectly funding the local Centre for Independent Living, which then pays attendants directly (Jones, 1987). This could be a reflection of the more general CIL philosophy beginning to influence or permeate practices in the areas where they are located.

There are different kinds of attendant care, ranging from the professional and formal care of nurses, to social services provision of home helps, to voluntary sector provision and informal family care. In the voluntary sector, organisations such as Crossroads and the Association of Carers have pioneered Care Attendant Schemes, sometimes also referred to as family support services. Most of these schemes provide respite care for the relatives of the person with the disability and thus only indirectly provide a service for the person with the disability. The aim of such schemes is generally to assist those who are caring for someone with a disability in their own homes and so prevent the breakdown of community care and the possibility of resulting institutionalisation. In this sense, these schemes are important in enabling greater independence, but they are rather more oriented towards carers than giving complete control to the disabled person to determine the type of assistance she or he requires. In a survey of schemes in Greater London, all schemes had the dual aim of supporting carers and enabling people with disabilities to maintain their dignity and independence in their own homes (GLAD, 1985). These voluntary sector schemes appear to be of particular importance to women, as the same survey found that two-thirds of both carers and clients were women. In some areas, three-quarters of the people with disabilities were women, although a survey of all Crossroads schemes found that 57 per cent of clients were women (Bristow, 1981).

Something like the *Århus* scheme could be especially helpful to women who are disabled. Mary Croxon John (1988, p. 131) suggests that given the greater difficulties women experience entering the labour market, the kind of support they receive and the training it gives them helps to redress the 'imbalance of disadvantage'. The same could equally be said in relation to the greater poverty and dependency experienced by women who are disabled. Attendant needs might also require some redefinition to include the needs of women who are disabled and have young children.

The Disabled Persons Act 1986

In contrast to an approach which stresses financial independence, a policy linking self-determination for people with disabilities with advocacy was adopted in Britain in 1986. At the end of 1985, a Bill was launched which aimed to give people with disabilities a greater say in decisions affecting their lives. It had the rather wordy title of the Disabled Persons (Services, Consultation and Representation) Bill, but was popularly dubbed the Tom Clarke Bill after its initiator, a Labour Member of Parliament from Scotland. Since becoming law, it is often simply referred to as the Disabled Persons Act 1986. It is a wide-ranging piece of legislation which, in eighteen sections, covers things such as local authority assessment procedures, the discharging of people from hospitals into the community, and assistance for carers. It is oriented towards three groups: young people leaving special education, people leaving long-stay hospitals (largely people with mental disabilities), and people living at home whose carers (usually elderly parents) can no longer cope.

While the Act is difficult and complex, it has one underlying message, namely that disabled people should have more say and control over their own lives (Bingley and Hurst, 1987). Its main thrust is advocacy. It gives people with disabilities the right and the power to appoint their own chosen representative to be present at all procedures in which their needs are assessed or examined, and to get a written record of all decisions taken about them. In addition to this, a central feature of the Act was a commitment to consult with organisations of disabled people (Clarke, 1986).

The Act was a Private Member's Bill which, in the context of British parliamentary procedure, meant that it could not order additional money to be earmarked for carrying out the requirements of the Act. In the light of this and the potentially high costs envisaged of implementing the Act, there has been considerable delay on the part of government ministers in the announcement of commencement orders giving dates for the various clauses of the Act. The lack of financial provision for implementing it has also led to the Act being criticised by local authorities, who have expressed reservations about legislation which 'laid down detailed, time-consuming and costly procedures for assessment, administration and record keeping' and the bureaucracy that this would involve. Whilst apparently supporting the objectives of the Act, some local authorities have pointed out that 'no one will get them simply by passing laws saying they have to happen, without also providing the resources needed to create them'. The cost of the new consultation and assessment procedures alone, without the increased services that would ensue, was originally estimated to be about £100 million in 1986 (Greaves, 1986). This was subsequently amended to £150 million by the Minister for Social Security and the Disabled (*Hansard*, 17 February 1987, col. 198).

The combination of a reluctant, cost-cutting government and financially pressured local authorities proved extremely serious for the implementation of the Act. Consequently, although the Act was supported by all political parties and passed by the House of Commons, by 1988 only a limited number of its eighteen clauses had been brought into force. Additionally, no information about the Act or the new procedures had been published or disseminated by government, raising doubts about the commitment of the Act to consult with disabled people. Local authorities, however, are obliged to consult organisations of people with disabilities before co-opting someone with special knowledge of the needs of disability to any forum. This represents a solid advance towards representation by people with disabilities, even though the remainder of the Act moves forward very slowly.

Advocacy can mean a number of different things. It can mean legal or other professional-type advocacy, and it can mean group or self-advocacy. The Disabled Persons Act 1986 emphasises individual advocacy either by self or by another person. Although representation under the Act has been taken largely to mean advocacy by a friend or professional in situations where the person concerned has an intellectual or communication disability, it also allows for self-representation. This right should not be lost as the person with the disability is best able to know how the disability effects his or her daily living and ambitions. While acknowledging that there may be a need for 'outside' help, it may not necessarily be appropriate for this to come from the local authority or health authority. Although there is nothing in the Act excluding officers of statutory bodies being representatives, this would be against the spirit of the Act. The intention of the Act is that the rights of the representative must always be subject to the wishes of the person being represented (Parratt, 1988).

Clearly this type of legislation represents a step in the direction of self-determination for people with disabilities. However, any piece of legislation is only as strong as the political will to pay for and enforce it (as was seen in the discussion of the quota scheme in Chapter 7). In addition, its real objectives can only be achieved if administrators are prepared to recognise that much legislation is guided by principles which are not always possible to enshrine in technically correct legal clauses. The spirit of the Disabled Persons Act 1986 was clearly to recognise and make provision for the rights of people with disabilities to determine the course of their own lives. Whether this aim will be fulfilled depends on the ability of able-bodied administrators and professionals to take a back seat and to facilitate the decisions of others, rather than attempt to control those decision themselves, and to acknowledge that people with disabilities have rights as well as needs.

Independence and self-determination are goals with which most people and most politicians can agree. Like policies of community care and self-help, they can be all things to all people. As slogans, they are rallying cries both for the populist disability movements demanding a slice of political power and for politicians wishing to reduce public spending by 'respectable' means. They are both responses to the power and control which professionals exert, as well as a means of questioning the appropriateness of statutory funding.

A distinction needs to be made between these two goals. Real self-determination entails more than a plea for equal opportunities in a market-based society which generates social divisions and in which inequality not only prevails but is the indispensable condition of that society. Calls for consumer power will ultimately amount to little if they are not backed by broader legislative and social change which leads to appropriate adjustments in the balance of economic resources.

This is especially true in relation to the position of women, for whom independence and greater control over their lives is linked to both an economic system which discriminates against them and a society which is deeply patriarchal. In addition, the pattern of disability for many women is one of disablement accompanied by chronic long-term illness, such as in arthritis and multiple sclerosis. For these women, therefore, independence and self-determination of necessity will require more than having a voice to assert their freedom to choose, however important that may be. Distributive justice for women depends on significant changes in the organisation of work, in the provision of income outside paid employment, in child care, and in the provision of a range of support services which are beyond the capacities of individuals operating in the market place. At present insufficient resources are being put into community services, the provision of basic aids and health care services. Adequate and satisfactory services are essential to make it possible for women with disabilities to become visible and independent, and to exert greater control over their lives.

Bibliography

Abberley, Paul (1987) 'The concept of oppression and the development of a social theory of disability', *Disability, Handicap and Society*, 2(1).

Ablon, Joan (1981a) 'Dwarfism and social identity: self-help group participation', *Social Science and Medicine*, 15B(1), January.

Ablon, Joan (1981b) 'Stigmatised health conditions', *Social Science and Medicine*, 15B(1).

Agerholm, Margaret (1975a) 'The identification and evaluation of long-term handicap', *The Medico-Legal Journal*, 43(4).

Agerholm, Margaret (1975b) 'Handicaps and the handicapped: a nomenclature and classification of intrinsic handicap', *Royal Society of Health Journal, 95(3)*.

Albeda, Wil (1985) *Disabled People and Their Employment*. Commission of the European Communities in co-operation with the European Centre for Work and Society.

Albrecht, Gary (ed.) (1976) *The Sociology of Physical Disability and Rehabilitation*, University of Pittsburgh Press.

Albrecht, Gary, *et al.* (1982) 'Social distance from the stigmatised: a test of two theories', *Social Science and Medicine*, 16.

Alcock, Pete (1987) *Poverty and State Support*. Longman.

Anderson, E.M. and Clarke, L. (1982) *Disability in Adolescence*, Methuen.

Anson, O. and Anson, J. (1986) 'Women's health and labour force status: an enquiry using a multi point measure of labour force participation', *Social Science and Medicine*, 25 (1).

Asch, Adrienne (1986) 'Will populism empower the disabled?', *Social Policy*, Winter.

Ashok, Hansa *et al.* (1985) *Home Sweet Work Station*, Greater London Council Equal Opportunities Group.

Asrael, Wilma (1982) 'An approach to motherhood for disabled women', *Rehabilitation Liberature*, 43 (7–8).

Atkins, Bobbie J. (1982) 'Vocational rehabilitation counseling for women: recommendations for the eighties', *Rehabilitation Literature* 43 (7–8).

Baldwin, Sally (1977) *Disabled Children – Counting the Costs*. Disability Alliance.

Baldwin, Sally (1985) *The Costs of Caring*, Routledge and Kegan Paul.

Barton, Len (1986) 'The politics of special educational needs', *Disability, Handicap and Society*, 1(3).

Battye, L. (1966) 'The Chatterley syndrome', in P. Hunt (ed.), *Stigma – The Experience of Disability*, Geoffrey Chapman.

Becker, Elle (1978) *Female Sexuality Following Spinal Cord Injury*, Accent Press.

Becker, Elle (1981) 'Sexuality and the spinal cord injured woman', in D. Bullard, and S. Knight, *op cit.*

Becker, Gaylene (1981) 'Coping with stigma: lifelong adaptation of deaf people', *Social Science and Medicine*, 15B(1).

Becker, H. (1963) *Outsiders*, Free Press.

Bingley, William and Hurst, Rachel (1987) *Getting in on the Act*, Thames Television.

Bisset, Liz and Huws, Ursula (1984) *Sweated Labour. Homeworking in Britain Today*. Low Pay Unit.

Blaxter, Mildred (1976) *The Meaning of Disability*, Heinemann Educational.

Bochel, Hugh and Taylor-Gooby, Peter (1986) 'Parliament and disability', *Rehab Network*, 3.

Bogdan, Robert and Taylor, Steve (1987) 'Towards a sociology of acceptance: the other side of the study of deviance', *Social Policy*, Fall.

Bogle, J.E. and Shaul, S.L. (1981) 'Body image and women', in D. Bullard and S. Knight, *op cit.*

Bone, M. and Meltzer, H. (1989) *The Prevalence of Disability among Children*, OPCS surveys of disability, Great Britain, Report 3, HMSO.

Bonwich, Emily (1985) 'Sex role attitudes and role reorganisation in spinal cord injured women', in M. Deegan and N. Brooks, (1985).

Bookis, Joan (1983) *Beyond the School Gate*. RADAR.

Borsay, Anne (1986) 'Personal trouble or public issue? Towards a model of policy for people with physical disabilities', *Disability, Handicap and Society*, 1(2).

Boswell, D.M. and Wingrove, J.M. (1974) *The Handicapped Person in the Community*, Tavistock.

Bowe, F. (1983) *Disabled Women in America: A Statistical Report Drawn From Census Bureau Data*, The President's Committee on Employment of the Handicapped.

Brechin, A. *et al.* (eds) (1981) *Handicap in a Social World*, Open University. Hodder and Stoughton.

Brisenden, Simon (1986) 'Independent living and the medical model of disability', *Disability, Handicap and Society*, 1(2).

Brisenden, Simon (1987) 'A response to 'Physical Disability in 1986 and Beyond': a report of the Royal College of Physicians', *Disability, Handicap and Society*, 2(2).

Bristow, A.K. (1981) *Crossroads Care Attendant Schemes. Study of Their Organisation and Working Practices and the Families Whom They Support.* Crossroads Care Attendant Schemes Ltd, Rugby.

Brittan, Yvonne (1982) 'The household income distribution of disabled people in the UK', *International Journal of Social Economics*, 9(6–7).

Brown, J.S. and Giesy, B. (1986) 'Marital status of persons with spinal cord injury', *Social Science and Medicine*, 23 (3).

Brown, Joan (1982) *Industrial Injuries*, Policy Studies Institute, no. 606.

Brown, Joan (1984) *The Disability Income System*, Policy Studies Institute, no. 626.

Brown, Joan and Small, Steven (1985) *Occupational Benefits as Social Security*, Policy Studies Institute.

Brown, J.S. and Rawlinson, M.E. (1972) 'Sex differences in sick role rejection and work performance following cardiac surgery', *Journal of Health and Social Behaviour*, 18.

Browne, Susan, E. *et al.* (eds) (1985) *With the Power of Each Breath*, Cleis Press.

Buckle, Judith (1971) *Work and Housing of Impaired Persons in Great Britain*, HMSO.

Buckle, Judith (1983) *Mental Handicap Costs More*, Disablement Income Group.

Bullard, D. and Knight, S. (eds) (1981) *Sexuality and Physical Disability: Personal Perspectives*, Mosby Publishers.

Burgess, Paul (1985) 'Keeping the lines open', *Community Care*, 8 August.

Burke, Gill (1981) *Housing and Social Justice*, Longman.

Bury, Michael R. (1979) 'Disablement in society: towards an integrated perspective', *International Journal of Rehabilitation Research*, 2(1).

Campling, Jo (1979) *Better Lives for Disabled Women*, Virago.

Campling, Jo (1981a) *Images of Ourselves: Women with Disabilities Talking*, Routledge and Kegan Paul.

Campling, Jo (1981b) 'Women and disability', in A. Walker and P. Townsend (eds) (1981).

Central Statistical Office (1986) *Social Trends*, 16, HMSO.

Clarke, T. (1986) 'A Bill to build with – money well spent', *Community Care*, 3 April.

Comer, R.J. and Piliavin, J.A. (1972) 'The effects of physical deviance upon face to face interaction: the other side', in D. Boswell and J. Wingrove, *op cit*.

Confederation of Indian Organisations (1988) *Double Bind: To Be Disabled and Asian*, CIO.

Cook, L. and Rossett, A. (1975) 'The sex role attitudes of deaf adolescent women and their implications for vocation choice', *American Annals of the Deaf*, 120.

CORAD (1982) Report by the Committee on Restrictions Against Disabled People, chaired by Peter Large, HMSO.

Coyle, A. (1984) *Redundant Women*, The Women's Press.

Coyle, A. and Skinner, J. (1988) *Women and Work*, Macmillan.

Croxon John, Mary (1988) *The Vocational Rehabilitation of Disabled Women in the European Community*, Report to the Commission of the EC.

Dailey, A.L.T. (1979) 'Physically handicapped women', *Counseling Psychologist*, 8.

Dartington, Tim *et al* (1981) *A Life Together*, Tavistock.

Davies, David and Scambler, Graham (1988) 'Attitudes towards epilepsy in general practice', *The International Journal of Social Psychiatry*, 34(1).

Davoud, Nicole (1980) *Part-time Employment, Time for Recognition, Organisation and Legal Reform*, RADAR and the Multiple Sclerosis Society.

Davoud, Nicole (1985) *Where do I go from here?* Judy Piatkus.

Davoud, Nicole and Kettle, Melvin (1980) *Multiple Sclerosis and its Effect upon Employment* Multiple Sclerosis Society.

Deegan, Mary Jo and Brooks, Nancy (eds) (1985) *Women and Disability*, Transaction Books

Deem, R. (1981) 'State policy and ideology in the education of women 1944–80', *British Journal of the Sociology of Education*, 2(2).

De Jong, G. (1981) 'The movement for independent living: origins, ideology and implications for disability research', in A. Brechin *et al.* (1981).

Derbyshire Coalition of Disabled People (DCDP) (1985) *Development of the Derbyshire Centre for Integrated Living*, selected papers.

Deshen, S. and Deshen, H. (1989) 'On social aspects of the usage of guide-dogs and long canes', *Sociological Review*, 37 (1).

Disability Alliance (1975) *Poverty and Disability: The Case for a Comprehensive Income Scheme for Disabled People*.

Disability Alliance (1987) *Poverty and Disability: Breaking the Link*.

Disability Alliance (1988) *Severe Disablement Allowance*.

Disablement Income Group (1974) *Realising a National Disability Income*.

Disablement Income Group (1979) *DIG's National Disability Income*.

Disablement Income Group (1987) *DIG's National Disability Income*.

Duckworth, D. (1983) *The Classification and Measurement of Disablement*, DHSS Research Report no. 10, HMSO.

Duffy, Yvonne (1981) *All Things Are Possible*, A.J. Garrin and Associates.

Durward, Lyn (1981) *That's the Way the Money Goes. The Extra Cost of Living with a Disability*, Disability Alliance.

Duval, M.L. (1984) 'Psychosocial metaphors of physical distress among multiple sclerosis patients', *Social Science and Medicine*, 19(6).

Earnshaw, Ian (1973) *Disabled Housewives on Merseyside*, Disablement Income Group.

Economist Intelligence Unit (1982) *Benefits for Partial Disability*, prepared for the Multiple Sclerosis Society of Great Britain and Northern Ireland.

Edwards, G. (1987) 'Anorexia and the family', in M. Lawrence, *Fed Up and Hungry*, The Women's Press.

European Community (1978) 'Directive of 19th December', *Official Journal of the European Communities*, No. L6/24, 10 January 1979.

Ferris, L.J. (1981) 'Being a disabled mother', in D. Bullard and S. Knight, (1981).

Fiedler, Barrie (1988) 'A fair slice of the cake', *Community Care*, 4 February.

Fine, M. and Asch, A. (1985) 'Disabled women: sexism without the pedestal', in M. Deegan and N. Brooks, (1985).

Finkelstein, V. (1980) *Attitudes and Disabled People*, World Rehabilitation Fund.

Fitzpatrick, R., Hinton, J., Newman, S., Scambler, G. and Thompson, J., (1984) *The Experience of Illness*, Tavistock.

Frank, G. (1984) 'Life history model of adaptation to disability: the case of a "congenital amputee"', *Social Science and Medicine*, 19(6).

Franklin, Paula A. (1977) 'Impact of disability on the family structure', *Social Security Bulletin*, May.

Furnham, A. and Pendred, J. (1983) 'Attitudes towards the mentally and physically disabled', *British Journal of Medical Psychology*, 56.

GLAD (1985) *Care Attendant Schemes, Their Management and Organisation*, Greater London Association for Disabled People.

GLC Women's Committee (1986) *Women and Disability*, Greater London Council Women's Committee Bulletin, 26.

Galluf Tate, Denise and Weston, Nancy Hanlon (1982) 'Women and disabilities: an international perspective', *Rehabilitation Literature*, 43(7–8).

Gething L. (1985) 'Perceptions of disability of persons with cerebral palsy, their close relatives, and able bodied persons', *Social Science and Medicine*, 20(6).

Gibson, G. and Ludwig, E.G. (1968) 'Family structure in a disabled population', *Journal of Marriage and the Family*, February.

Ginsburg, N. (1983) 'Home ownership and socialism in Britain: a bulwark against Bolshevism', *Critical Social Policy*, 7.

Glendinning, C. (1980) *After Working All These Years*, Disability Alliance.

Glendinning, C. and Baldwin, S. (1988) 'The costs of disability', in R. Walker and G. Parker, *Money Matters*, Sage.

Glendinning, C. and Miller, J. (1987) *Women and Poverty*, Wheatsheaf.

Goffman, E. (1968) *Stigma*, Prentice-Hall.

Greaves, Tony (1986) 'A Bill to build with – who pays?', *Community Care*. 3 April.

Greenblum, Joseph (1977) 'Effect of vocational rehabilitation on employment and earnings of the disabled: state variations', *Social Security Bulletin*, December.

Guttman, L. (1964) 'The married life of paraplegics and tetraplegics', *Paraplegia*, October.

Haavio-Mannila, Elina (1986) 'Inequalities in health and gender', *Social Science and Medicine*, 2(2).

Hahn, Harlan (1988) 'Can disability be beautiful?', *Social Policy*, Winter.

Hakim, C. (1978) 'Sexual divisions within the labour force: occupational segregation', *Employment Gazette*, 86(11).

Hakim, C. (1981) 'Job segregation: trends in the 1970s', *Employment Gazette*.

Hannaford, Susan (1985) *Living Outside Inside*, Berkeley, Canterbury Press.

Hardiker, Pauline *et al.* (1986) 'Coping with chronic renal failure', *British Journal of Social Work*, 16.

Hargreaves, D.J. and Colley, A.M. (eds) (1986) *The Psychology of Sex Roles*, Harper and Row.

Harris, A. (1971) *Handicapped and Impaired in Great Britain*, Office of Population Censuses and Surveys, HMSO.

Harris, A. *et al.* (1972) *Income and Entitlement to Supplementary Benefit of Impaired People in Great Britain*, OPCS, HMSO.

Harris, Margaret (1986) 'Hearing loss and family life', *Community Care.* 27 February.

Haveman, Robert H. *et al.* (1984) *Public Policy towards Disabled Workers: Cross-national Analysis of Economic Impacts*, Cornell University Press.

Hayslip, Josephine Buck (1981) *Developing Career Mobility for Women with Physical Disabilities*, unpublished dissertation.

Hermans, Pieter C. (1988) 'Differentials in the outcome of the application of the Dutch disability insurance legislation to women and men', *International Social Security Review*, 3.

Hill, C. (1969) *Reformation to Industrial Revolution*, Pelican.

Hillyer Davis, B. (1984) 'Women, disability and feminism: notes towards a new theory', *Frontiers*, 8(1).

Hillyer Davis, B. (1985) 'Disabled women: speaking for ourselves', *The Women's Review of Books*, 111 (2), November.

Hopper, Susan (1981) 'Diabetes as a stigmatised condition: the case of low income clinic patients in the United States', *Social Science and Medicine*, 15B (1).

Hunt, Paul (1966) *Stigma: The Experience of Disability*, Geoffrey Chapman.

Hurstfield, J. (1979) *The Part-Time Trap*, Low Pay Unit.

Hyman, M. (1977) *The Extra Costs of Disabled Living*, National Fund for Research into Crippling Diseases.

International Rehabilitation Review (1985) 'Women and disability: an overview of developments', IRR, Second trimester.

Jeffreys, M. *et al.* (1969) 'A set of tests for measuring motor impairment in prevalence studies', *Chronic Diseases*, 22, 5.

Jenkins, A.E. and Amos, O.C. (1983) 'Being black and disabled', *Journal of Rehabilitation*, April – June.

Jennings, S. Mazaik, C. and McKinlay, S. (1984) 'Women and Work: an investigation of the association between health and employment status in middle aged women', *Social Science and Medicine* 19,4.

John, Mary (1988) 'Women with disabilities, *Rehab Network*, 11, Autumn.

Jones, Derek (ed.) (1987) *Same Difference*, Channel 4 publication.

Jones, Trevor *et al.* (1988) *An Evaluation of Sheltered Placement Schemes*, Department of Employment.

Keirs, Jackie (1986) *A Change of Rhythm*, Headway (National Head Injuries Association), Nottingham.

Knudson-Cooper, Mary S. (1981) 'Adjustment to visible stigma: the case of the severely burned', *Social Science and Medicine*, 15B(1).

Kolb, C. (1981) 'Assertivenessness training for women with visual impairments', *Journal of Sociology and Social Welfare*, 8(2).

Korer, J. and Fitzsimmons, J.S. (1985) 'The effect of Huntington's Chorea on family life', *British Journal of Social Work*: 15.

Kutner, Nancy G. (1984) 'Women with disabling health conditions: the significance of employment', *Women and Health*, 9 (4).

Kutner, Nancy G. (1987) 'Social ties, social support, and perceived health status among chronically disabled people', *Social Science and Medicine*, 25 (1).

Kutner, N.G. and Gray, H.L. (1981) 'Women and chronic renal failure: some neglected issues', *Journal of Sociology and Social Welfare*, (8) 2.

Kutner, N. and Kutner, M. (1979) 'Race and sex as variables affecting reactions to disability', *Archives of Physical and Medical Rehabilitation*, 60.

Kutza, E.A. (1981) 'Benefits for the disabled: how beneficial for women?', *Journal of Sociology and Social Welfare*, 8(2).

Large, Peter (1988) 'DIG in Parliament', *Progress*, 15, Autumn.

Layard, R., Piachaud, D. and Stewart, M. (1978) 'The causes of poverty', Background Paper No. 5 to Report No. 6, *Lower Incomes*, Royal Commission on the Distribution of Income and Wealth, HMSO.

Lawrence, M. (1987) *Fed Up and Hungry*, The Women's Press.

Levitan, S.A. and Taggart, R. (1977) *Jobs for the Disabled* John Hopkins University Press.

Loach, Irene (1976) *The Price of Deafness*, Disability Alliance.

Locker, D. (1983) *Disability and Disadvantage*, Tavistock.

Longmore, Paul K. (1985) 'Screening stereotypes: images of disabled people', *Social Policy*, Summer.

Lonsdale, Susan (1981) *Job Protection for the Disabled*, Low Pay Unit.

Lonsdale, Susan (1985) *Work and Inequality*, Longman.

Lonsdale, Susan (1987) 'Patterns of paid work', in C. Glendinning and J. Millar, (1987).

Lonsdale, Susan and Byrne, Dominic (1988) 'Social security: from state insurance to private uncertainty', in M. Brenton and C. Ungerson, *Yearbook of Social Policy 1987–8*, Longman.

Lonsdale, Susan and Walker, Alan (1984) *A Right to Work: Disability and Employment*, Low Pay Unit.

Maccaby, E.M. and Jacklin, C.N. (1974) *The Psychology of Sex Differences*, Stanford University Press.

Manning, Nick and Oliver, Mike (1985) Madness, epilepsy and medicine in N. Manning (ed.) *Social Problems and Welfare Ideology*, Gower.

Manpower Services Commission (1981) *Employment Rehabilitation*, HMSO.

Manpower Services Commission (1982) *Review of Assistance for Disabled People*, HMSO.

Manpower Services Commission (1984) *Proposals for the Development of the Manpower Services Commission's Rehabilitation Service: A Report to the Commission*, HMSO.

Marcus, Alfred *et al.* (1981) 'Sex differences in reports of illness and disability: a further test of the fixed role hypothesis, *Social Science and Medicine*, 17 (15).

Marinelli, Robert P. and Dell Orto, Arthur E. (1977) *The Psychological and Social Impact of Physical Disability*, Springer Publishing Company.

Martin, J., Meltzer, H. and Elliot, D. (1988) *The Prevalence of Disability among Adults*, OPCS surveys of disability in Great Britain, Report 1, HMSO.

Martin, J. and White, A. (1988) *The Financial Circumstances of Disabled Adults Living in Private Households*, OPCS surveys of disability in Great Britain, Report 2, HMSO.

Martin, J., White, A. and Meltzer, H. (1989) *Disabled Adults: Services, Transport and Employment*, OPCS surveys of disability in Great Britain, Report 4, HMSO.

Martin, J. and Roberts, C. (1984) *Women and Employment: A Lifetime Perspective*, Office of Population Censuses and Surveys, HMSO.

Mason, M. (1985) 'Welcome Lucy Rose, in from the cold', *Liberation Network Journal*.

Matthews, Gwyneth F. (1983) *Voices from the Shadows: Women with Disabilities Speak Out*, Toronto, The Women's Press.

McKnight, J. (1981) 'Professionalised service and disabling help', in A. Brechin *et al.*, (1981).

Melville, Joy (1986) 'Sitting pretty', *New Society*, 14 March.

Miller, E.J. and Gwynne, G.V. (1972) *A Life Apart*, Tavistock.

Mitchell, Joyce S. (1980) *See Me Clearly: Career and Life Planning for Teens with Physical Disabilities*, Harcourt Brace Jovanovich.

Mitchell, J.N. (1981) 'Multiple sclerosis and the prospects for employment', *Journal of Social and Occupational Medicines*, 31.

Morgan, M. *et al.* (1984) 'Social networks and psychological support among disabled people', *Social Science and Medicine*, 19 (5).

Mudrick, N.R. (1983a) 'Disabled women', *Society* 20 (3).

Mudrick, N. (1983b) 'Notes on policy and practice. Income support programmes for disabled women', *Social Service Review*; March.

Mudrick, N. (1987) 'Differences in receipt of rehabilitation by impaired midlife men and women', *Rehabilitation Psychology*, 32(1).

NACEDP (1983) *Report of the Working Party on Homeworkers*, National Advisory Council on Employment of Disabled People, April

Nathan, Susan W. (1977) 'Body images of scoliotic female adolescents before and after surgery', *Maternal-Child-Nursing Journal*, 6(3), Fall.

Nathanson, C.A. (1980) 'Social roles and health status among women: the significance of employment', *Social Science and Medicine*, 14.

National Audit Office (1987) *Department of Employment and Manpower Services Commission: Employment Assistance to Disabled Adults*, HMSO.

National Childbirth Trust (1984) *The Emotions and Experiences of Some Disabled Mothers*, NCT.

Neistadt, M. and Baker, M.F. (1978) 'A program for sex counseling the physically disabled', *American Journal of Occupational Therapy*, 32(10).

Newman, S.P. (1984a) 'The psychological consequences of cerebrovascular accident and head injury', in R. Fitzpatrick *et al.*, (1984).

Newman, S.P. (1984b) 'Anxiety, hospitalisation and surgery', in R. Fitzpatrick *et al.*, (1984).

Nissel, M. and Bonnerjea, L. (1982) *Family Care of the Handicapped Elderly: Who Pays?*, Policy Studies Institute.

Occupational Pensions Board (1977) *Occupational Pension Scheme Cover for Disabled People.* Cmnd 6849, HMSO.

O'Donovan, K. and Szyszczak, E. (1988) *Equality and Sex Discrimination Law* Basil Blackwell.

Office of Health Economics (1977) *Physical Impairment: Social Handicap.*

O'Leary, J. (1983) 'Disabled women and employment', *Rehabilitation Digest*, 14 (3), Canada.

Oliver, M. (1983) *Social Work with Disabled People*, Macmillan.

Oliver, M. (1984) 'The politics of disability', *Critical Social Policy*, 11.

Oliver, M. (1986) 'Social policy and disability: some theoretical issues', *Disability, Handicap and Society*, 1(1).

O'Toole, J. and Weeks, C. (1978) *What Happens after School? A Study of Disabled Women and Education*, Women's Educational Equity Communications Network, San Francisco.

OUTSET (1983) *The OUTSET Paradigm of Handicap.*

OUTSET (1986a) *Disability, Handicap and Housing in Haringey.*

OUTSET (1986b) *Action on Disability Survey in Milton Keynes.*

OUTSET (1987a) *Public Attitudes towards Disabled People.*

OUTSET (1987b) *Summary of Methodologies for the Conduct of Surveys of Disabled People.*

Oyer, E.J. and Paolucci, B. (1970) 'Homemakers' hearing losses and family integration', *Journal of Home Economics* 62(4), April.

Palmer, C. and Poulton, K. (1987) *Sex and Race Discrimination in Employment, Legal Action Group.*

Parratt, David (1988) *Act Now*, Royal Association for Disability and Rehabilitation.

Passanante, M.R. and Nathanson, C.A. (1985) 'Female labor force participation and female mortality in Wisconsin 1974–1978', *Social Science and Medicine*, 21(6).

Perlman, L. and Arneson, K. (1982) *Women and the Rehabilitation of Disabled Persons*, Report of the Mary Switzer 6th Memorial seminar, National Rehabilitation Association, USA.

Perry, Deborah (1984) *More Equal than Some*, Lady Margaret Hall Settlement.

Public Accounts Committee (1988) *Employment Assistance to Disabled Adults*, House of Commons, Twenty-first Report, HMSO.

Quicke, John (1985) *Disability in Modern Children's Fiction*, Croom Helm.

Rees, Jessica (1983) *Sing a Song of Silence*, Kensal Press.

Robbins, Diana (1982) *The Chance to Work. Improving Employment Prospects for Disabled People.* Disablement Income Group.

Robinson, Ian (1988) *Multiple Sclerosis*, Tavistock.

Romano, Mary D. (1978) 'Sexuality and the disabled female', *Sexuality and Disability*, (1)1, Spring.

Royal College of Physicians (1986a) 'Physical disability in 1986 and beyond', *Journal of the Royal College of Physicians of London*, 20(3).

Royal College of Physicians (1986b) *The Young Disabled Adult*, RCP.

Royal National Institute for the Deaf (1987) *Communication Works: An RNID Inquiry into the Employment of Deaf People*, RNID.

Ryerson, Ellen (1981) 'Sexual abuse of disabled persons and prevention alternatives', in D. Bullard and S. Knight, (1981).

Safilios-Rothschild, Constantina (1970) *The Sociology and Social psychology of Disability and Rehabilitation*, Random House.

Safilios-Rothschild, Constantina (1977) 'Discrimination against disabled women', *International Rehabilitation Review*, 2(4).

Sainsbury, S. (1970) *Registered as Disabled*, G. Bell and Sons.

Sainsbury, S. (1973) *Measuring Disability*, G. Bell and Sons.

Saviola, Marilyn (1981) 'Personal reflections on physically disabled women and dependency', *Professional Psychology*, 12(1).

Saxton, Marsha (1981) 'A peer counseling training program for disabled women', *Journal of Sociology and Social Welfare*, 8(2).

Scambler, G. (1984) 'Perceiving and coping with stigmatising illness', in R. Fitzpatrick *et al.*, (1984).

Schuster, Jan D. and Kelly, Donice H. (1974) 'Preferred style features in dresses for physically handicapped elderly women', *The Gerontologist*, April.

Scotch, Richard K. (1985) *From Good Will to Civil Rights, Transforming Federal Disability Policy*, Temple University Press.

Scott, Robert (1969) *The Making of Blind Men*, Russell Sage Foundation.

Scott, Robert A. (1970) 'The construction of conceptions of stigma by professional experts', in Jack D. Douglas (ed.) *Deviance and Respectability: The Social Construction of Moral Meanings*. Basic Books.

Seattle Rape Relief (1979) *Information Concerning Sexual Exploitation of Mentally and Physically Handicapped Individuals*, Developmental Disabilities Project, Seattle Rape Relief Project, Washington.

Segal, Audrey (1986) 'Push for power', *New Society*, 25 April.

Shaul, S., Bogle, J.E., Norman, A. and Hale-Harbaugh, J. (1978) *Towards Intimacy: Family Planning and Sexuality Concerns of Physically Disabled Women*, Human Sciences Press.

Shearer, Ann (1981a) *Disability: Whose Handicap?*, Basil Blackwell.

Shearer, Ann (1981b) 'A framework for independent living', in A. Walker and P. Townsend, *Disability in Britain. A Manifesto of Rights*, Martin Robertson.

Shearer, Ann (1982) *Living Independently*, Centre on Environment for the Handicapped and the King's Fund Centre.

Shelter (1988) *Freedom to Lose: Housing Policy and People with disabilities.*

Social Security Advisory Committee (SSAC) (1988) *Benefits for Disabled People: A Strategy for Change*, HMSO.

Somerville, Paula (1980) *Women in Employment Rehabilitation Centres*, Employment Rehabilitation Research Centre, Information Paper no. 7, HMSO.

Spastics Society (1985) *Discrimination and Disabled People.*

Spastics Society (1986) *An Equal Chance for Disabled People. A Study of Discrimination in Employment.*

Stace, Sheila (1986) *Vocational Rehabilitation for Women with Disabilities*, International Labour Office.

Stone, Deborah (1984) *The Disabled State*, Macmillan.

Stubbins, J. (1981) *Resettlement Services of the Employment Services, Manpower Services Commission: Some Observations*, in A. Brechin *et al.*, (1981).

Sutherland, Allan T. (1981) *Disabled We Stand*, Souvenir Press.

Task Force on Concerns of Physically Disabled Women (1978) *Within Reach*, Human Sciences Press.

Tawny, R.H. (1926) *Religion and the Rise of Capitalism*, Penguin.

Thane, P. (1982) *The Foundations of the Welfare State*, Longman.

Thomas, David (1982) *The Experience of Handicap*, Methuen.

Thompson, P. (1987) 'Perceptions of inequality', *Progress*, 13, Summer.

Thompson, P. *et al.* (1988) *Not the OPCS survey*, Disablement Income Group.

Thornton, Carla E. (1981) 'Sexuality counseling of women with spinal cord injuries', in D. Bullard and S. Knight, (1981).

Thurer, Shari L. (1982) 'Women and rehabilitation', *Rehabilitation Literature*, 43 (7–8).

Titley, Robert W. and Viney, Wayne (1969) 'Expression of aggression towards the physically handicapped', *Perceptual and Motor Skills*, 29.

Topliss, E. (1979) *Provision for the Disabled*, Basil Blackwell.

Townsend, P. (1979) *Poverty in the United Kingdom*, Penguin.

Union of the Physically Impaired Against Segregation (1975) *Fundamental Principles of Disability*, UPIAS and Disability Alliance.

US Department of Health and Human Services, Social Security Administration, Office of Policy (1982) *1978 Survey of Disabled and Work: Data Book*; Washington DC, Government Publishing Office.

Vash, Caroline (1982) 'Employment issues for women with disabilities', *Rehabilitation Literature*, 43 (7–8).

Victor, C.R. and Vetter, N.J. (1986) 'Poverty, disability and use of services by the elderly: analysis of the 1980 General Household Survey', *Social Science and Medicine*, 22(10).

Viney, Linda L. and Westbrook, Mart T. (1982) 'Patterns of anxiety in the chronically ill', *British Journal of Medical Psychology*, 55.

Viney, L. and Westbrook, M. (1984) 'Coping with chronic illness: strategy preferences, changes in preferences and associated emotional reactions', *Journal of Chronic Diseases*, 37 (6).

Walker, Alan and Townsend, Peter (1981) *Disability in Britain A Manifesto of Rights*, Martin Robertson.

Walker, Alan (1981) 'Assessing the severity of disability for the allocation of benefits and services', *International Social Security Review*, 34(3).

Walker, R. and Parker, G. (1988) *Money Matters*, Sage.

Ward, Sue (1986) *The Government's Pension Proposals: Their Effect on Disabled People*, unpublished paper.

Weinberg-Asher, Nancy (1976) 'The effect of physical disability on self-perception', *Rehabilitation Counselling Bulletin*, September.

Weir, S. (1981) 'Our image of the disabled, and how ready we are to help', *New Society*, 1 January.

Weitzman, Leonore J. (1979) *Sex Role Socialisation*, Mayfield Publishing Company, California.

Wickham, Ann (1982) 'The state and training programmes for women', in *The Experience of Women*, The Open University/Martin Robertson.

Wood, P.H.N. (1978) 'The young chronic sick', *Journal of the Royal Society of Medicine*, 71, June.

World Health Organisation (1980) *International Classification of Impairments, Disabilities and Handicaps*, WHO.

Zeldow, P.B. and Pavlou, M. (1984) 'Physical disability, life stress and psychosocial adjustment in multiple sclerosis', *Journal of Nervous and Mental Disease*, 172(2).

Index